Children of Immortal Bliss

A New Perspective on Our True Identity
based on the Ancient Vedanta Philosophy of India

PAUL HOURIHAN
Edited by Anna Hourihan

Vedantic Shores Press
Redding, CA

Published by: Vedantic Shores Press
                  P.O. Box 493100
                  Redding, CA 96049
                  info@vedanticshorespress.com
                  http://www.VedanticShoresPress.com.

First Printing 2008. Printed and bound in the U.S.A.
Second Printing 2008. Printed in the U.S.A. on recycled paper (30% PCW).

The OM symbol on the front cover and title page is based on the Shanti Sadan OM and is reproduced by permission of Shanti Sadan, London (www.shantisadan.org).

Publisher's Cataloging-in-Publication
(Provided by Quality Books, Inc.)

Hourihan, Paul.
   Children of immortal bliss : a new perspective on our
true identity based on the ancient Vedanta philosophy of
India / Paul Hourihan ; edited by Anna Hourihan. — 1st
ed.
   p. cm.
   Includes bibliographical references and index.
   LCCN 2003117047
   ISBN-13: 978-1-931816-08-3
   ISBN-10: 1-931816-08-5

   1. Vedanta. 2. Self (Philosophy)—India.
I. Hourihan, Anna. II. Title.

   B132.V3H68 2008   181'.48
                          QBI07-600240

Children of Immortal Bliss is humbly dedicated to the swamis of the Ramakrishna Order of India who left their beloved land to come to the West, and who stand as exemplars of the great Vedantic tradition. Following in the footsteps of Swami Vivekananda, they have carried on the vital work to bring these liberating teachings here where we have so much need of them.

ACKNOWLEDGMENTS:

We gratefully acknowledge permission to use excerpts from the following:
The Upanishads, Breath of the Eternal, trans. Swami Prabhavananda and Frederick Manchester. Copyright © 1947, 1957 by the Vedanta Society of Southern California. *The Song of God: Bhagavad-Gita,* trans. Swami Prabhavananda and Christopher Isherwood, Vedanta Press. Copyright © 1944, 1951 by the Vedanta Society of Southern California, www.Vedanta.com.
The Teachings of the Mystics, Walter T. Stace, Mentor/New American Library. Copyright © 1960, by the Estate of W. T. Stace.
The Upanishads, trans. Eknath Easwaran of the Blue Mountain Center of Meditation. Copyright © 1987. The Upanishad quotation on the back cover is reprinted by permission of Nilgiri Press, P. O. Box 256, Tomales, CA 94971, www.easwaran.org.
Christian scriptural quotations are taken from the King James version of the *Holy Bible*.

The Editor would like to acknowledge the contributions of the following individuals:
I am very grateful to the friends and colleagues who took the time and trouble to help me during the various stages of the editing process. Friends who kindly read an early version of this text and whose responses led to an improved and more comprehensive study: Marianne, Ralph, Nick and especially Durga who read the early and later versions of the book. My thanks and appreciation to Kim for her valuable editorial services and general advice, whose work helped make the material more accessible to a broader audience. Thanks also to Bruce for his useful editorial comments and Ana and Susana for their capable proofreading skills. And finally, my deep gratitude to Mahadevi for her support and helpful suggestions during the production phase and for dedicating a significant amount of time to creating a beautiful and uplifting cover design.

EDITOR'S NOTE

Vedanta in modern times is memorably linked with the celebrated Indian mystic Ramakrishna (1836–1886) and his renowned disciple Swami Vivekananda (1863–1902). Many of the insights in the pages to follow have been gleaned from a close study of the lives and works of these preeminent souls.

This presentation is intended to convey the core concepts of the Vedantic thought of India and therefore the emphasis is on its philosophy rather than India's rich cultural wellsprings that can be studied elsewhere.

The material for this text was derived from the author's original course notes and lectures given at the University of Guelph, School of Continuing Studies, in Ontario, Canada. The purpose of the lectures was to introduce Vedantic ideas to Westerners and this orientation is carried over into the present text. It has been recast for a reading rather than a listening audience.

The author's hope and prayer was that the ideas, insights, and promising message of these profound scriptures of India will inspire and encourage the reader to personally test the validity of these universal truths.

It is also hoped that *Children of Immortal Bliss* will serve as a reminder to India's own sons and daughters, especially those in the West, of her invaluable spiritual legacy to the world.

– A.H.

CONTENTS

PREFACE

The philosophy of Vedanta is as profound and mysterious as India, the ancient country of its origin. India, a land with unknown beginnings, is a suitable home for such a timeless philosophy.

As we are truly becoming a global village, the universal message of Vedanta's main principles increasingly resonates with the world at large. Particularly since it stresses the universal truths common to all religions instead of the differences that divide them, its teachings are indispensable to a world fragmented by opposing beliefs, where these apparent differences are causing endless strife, conflict, and war.

The core Vedantic ideas of unity of existence, universality of religious truth and our indwelling divine nature no longer seem as strange to us as they did only 75 or 100 years ago when the general belief was that God was distant, in His heaven, and "the judge of the earth." Many in the West who want a better under-standing of God in human affairs no longer subscribe to this model, but feel that God may not be so distant after all. This is a momentous step forward. These and other related beliefs have been slowly filtering into Western consciousness, principally through the influence of Vedanta and other Eastern wisdom teachings.

An important example of this subtle influence may be seen in our political thinking. The ideal of democracy was unknown, even in the West, just over two centuries ago. So democracy is a rare flowering of political institutions, perhaps achieving its best statement in the Declaration of Independence, powerfully expressed in Thomas Jefferson's words:

> We hold these truths to be self-evident that all men are created equal, that they are endowed by their Creator with certain unalienable rights and that among these are life, liberty, and the pursuit of happiness.

One wonders how Jefferson, an advanced thinker of his time, was inspired by these concepts, which clearly reflect Vedantic principles. Those truths were *not* self-evident to the mass of humanity then, and to much of it even today. On the other hand, the principle of spiritual democracy — of the divine presence dwelling in all beings — is self-evident to the mystic and the Vedantist.

Swami Vivekananda, the great modern expounder of Vedanta philosophy, spent four years of his short life in the United States. Significantly, after returning to India, he chose to leave his physical body on July 4, 1902, in tribute, we believe, to the American ideals as expressed in the Declaration.

Still, we may ask, what's the use of this knowledge? How can we possibly apply the insights of these ancient teachings in our day-to-day lives? This knowledge is of great use. We have to know what the Truth, the highest principle is in order to be guided by it during our long voyage over the seas of life. Then, though we may falter many times, we look up, and like the North Star, it is there, guiding us back to the path. Gradually, we begin to incorporate something of the spiritual power of that Truth into the texture of our lives.

Consciousness is Brahman....

He through whom man sees, tastes, smells, hears, and enjoys is verily the immortal Self....

There are two selves, the apparent and the real. Of these it is the real Self, and He alone, who must be felt as truly existing....

He who sees all beings in the Self and the Self in all beings hates none....

This Self is Brahman.

– Upanishads

PART ONE

The Mysticism of India

-An Overview-

1

Introduction

India, the country shaped like a heart, is the mystical heart of the world. It is the great reservoir of spirituality for humanity to dip into whenever it tires of the aridity of secular life and materialism, of doctrines and sensuality. Since its precious teachings have been translated and given away to the rest of the world over the last two centuries, perhaps it isn't as necessary now to go to India to discover them: India is a spiritual territory, a spiritual direction, not a geography. So in this text we will try to capture the spirit of India—the India of the sages, of lofty thoughts, of the highest mysticism—and the essence of that is called Vedanta.

Vedanta is one of the six main schools of philosophy in Hinduism. We don't hear very much about the other systems of thought in the West because they are not as exportable, not universal enough to have made the passage to the West. Only Vedanta and Yoga have successfully made the passage from India to the West. These are the most fascinating and useful to us and will be our focus.

The Vedanta philosophy consists chiefly of several great works: the Upanishads, the *Bhagavad Gita,* and the Brahma or Vedanta Sutras. This philosophy is like the manor house that you find in certain countries like England. To the original house various wings and annexes have been constructed over time until it becomes a vast sprawling collection of outbuildings. But the original manor house is still distinct—we can see that that is where it all started, because all the other buildings flow from it. So likewise the Upanishads represent the manor house of Vedanta, which includes many annexes.

The Vedanta system of thought is unique in its unequivocal approach to Truth. It postulates the following:

- Nothing exists except the Divine Being, or *Brahman*, as it is called in Hinduism. As the essence of all, it pervades, supports, and explains everything. The doctrine of the Spiritual Oneness of Existence follows from this.

- *Truth is One; Sages call it by different names.* Prophets differ in their interpretation of religion due to their cultural backgrounds, and the need of the people, but not in the essentials, so that the various religions are different paths to the same goal.

- The very nature of the Soul is divine: the Cosmic Self manifests as the individual Self or *Atman* as it is called in Hinduism. Therefore, as heirs to the Divine Self, we truly are all *Children of Immortal Bliss.*

- The primary goal in life is to realize, through direct personal experience, the divine nature within our own self.

Hinduism keeps growing. It is not completed, but is open-ended—by its nature it had no beginning and has no end. No one person founded it. Every other faith, religion, or cult has been founded by an individual who established the principles of that religion. But one of the many unique features of Hinduism is that it has had not one divine incarnation, or *avatar,* but many on which the philosophy of Hinduism was built. Their pantheon of supermystics includes such famous names as Rama, the most ancient of these, and Krishna, the most well known, and many more, including Buddha.

Buddha was raised a Hindu, and was a Hindu all his life, except for his later years when he became a reformer and founded a new faith called Buddhism. One could say Buddhism is the major sect of Hinduism; it has much in common with Hinduism, just as Protestantism and Catholicism are more alike than not.

Rama, Krishna, and Buddha have been and are worshiped by millions of people worldwide. These avatars testify to the emphasis on the personal aspect of Hinduism. There have been many others—for example, Shankara, who lived sometime between the sixth and eighth centuries AD. He was one of the chief commentators of the nondualistic or *advaita* Vedanta, and the formulator of Hinduism as we know it today. He was an overpowering intellectual who drew on the long Vedic tradition that was even in his time many centuries old. Shankara was the philosopher who pulled all the vital ancient ideas together to reveal the tremendous spiritual heritage of India. He spent his short, dazzling life writing commentaries on the *Bhagavad Gita* and the Upanishads, as well as writing independent works. To this day he is the authority for interpreting Vedanta.

Vedanta accepts the personal God, although its approach is essentially impersonal. Divine incarnations are considered embodiments of the universal and eternal truths of Vedanta.

Another implicit tenet of Vedanta is reincarnation. To awaken, manifest, and realize the divinity that is our nature is not a task for one lifetime, but for many. (See more on reincarnation in Part II, p. 46, "The Wheel of Karma.")

India has always produced great sages. Despite its heavy emphasis on principles, on spiritual law, and on mysticism, it is
India: Land of the Sages the land of the *rishis*, the ancient Hindu seers to whom was revealed the knowledge of the Vedas. In every century India produces three or four spiritual giants. They have an endless list of saints, and sages—women and men alike. The twentieth century has produced Ramana Maharshi, the renowned Advaitist who emphasized self-inquiry, and Sri Aurobindo, who was a brilliant scholar, activist, and mystic who formulated the Integral Yoga philosophy that incorporates concepts from both Western and Eastern philosophies. The nineteenth century gave us Swami Vivekananda and his teacher, the celebrated saint (or avatar, as some believe) Sri Ramakrishna. Vivekananda played a pivotal role in bringing the ideas of Vedanta to the West.

Mahatma Gandhi, the great religious and political leader, is another name we are all familiar with. Although he was not strictly speaking in the mystical tradition, he was a great soul, as his title "Mahatma" indicates. It is fitting that India required a religious leader for its independence. In other words, only a mahatma, and not merely a political leader, could capture the imagination of India and lead its people to self-governance.

India's ancient culture and much of her civilization—especially
The Importance of Sanskrit her classical language, Sanskrit—are religiously oriented. Sanskrit is the

ancient language in which the Vedas, the earliest Hindu scriptures, were written. Sanskrit is a language that developed chiefly to express religious thought, unlike Latin, Greek, and other classical languages of other early cultures. Sanskrit is not a spoken language, but it has an immense prestige in India to this day. You have to learn Sanskrit, so to speak, if you want to be considered a thinker or a scholar in India. Naturally, the yogis and the mystics know Sanskrit, too, because of the reverence for the language in which the scriptures were written.

So from her earliest times, India had a unique language. Her Vedic scriptures in Sanskrit have been handed down through the ages in an almost flawless transmission.[*] India has the oldest unbroken mystical tradition in the world. It is the only country that has had such a longstanding tradition.

The Hindu Scriptures

Strangely, the Hindu scriptures that many of us in the West have found so valuable are not read by the majority of Hindus. Those who do read them are the scholars, pundits, mystics, would-be mystics, and philosophers. Hindus have their own popular religion, as do people everywhere. They show reverence to their scriptures and

---

[*] Western scholars of ancient texts of India determined that these teachings were transmitted orally almost perfectly for vast stretches of time. When these teachings were finally rendered in prose or in verse for the first time, about the time of Christ or a few centuries before then, they represented the most perfect transmission of the material that has been found anywhere in any other tradition. These Western scholars, who may not have had any special interest in Hinduism, couldn't account for this. Why was the oral rendering almost flawless over many centuries? Because of the reverence for the teaching in the transmission. The transmitters must have conveyed that every word was priceless.

genuflect before them from a distance, but don't actually read them. Even illiterate people bow down in worship to the Upanishads and the *Bhagavad Gita.* They can't read them, but they know the stories and the teachings because they have heard them and they feel that somehow these scriptures represent everything. Perhaps they can't follow all the teachings in their daily lives, but in a way they are beginning to bring them to life by their veneration. Like ordinary people everywhere, they don't have either the time, the strength, the development, or the circumstances to go deeply into religious thought—that is always a pursuit for the few in the East, as well as the West. So there are large numbers of Hindus who do read them—but in a country of over a billion, these are relatively few.

The original meaning of *upanishad* is a secret teaching or doctrine communicated by a teacher to a chosen disciple who is sitting nearby—a teaching, therefore, that is imbibed from close contact. What the ordinary Hindu may sense is that these teachings of Vedanta—the Upanishads, the *Bhagavad Gita,* and the Brahma Sutras, along with the *Yoga Sutras*—are secret teachings and always have been felt to be such. The translation of these documents into many Western languages and into the major languages of India such as Hindi, Tamil, Telugu, Urdu, and Bengali, has been a relatively recent phenomenon that started about 200 years ago.

The Brahma or Vedanta Sutras are another important part of the Vedantic structure. They present the Vedantic teachings in a logical and methodical order.

The people have their own scriptures too; the chief ones are the Puranas. In the Puranas and in similar devotional works the lives of their great heroes, saints, sages, and legends are captured in beautiful verse and prose. There are many valuable teachings here that have been distilled out of the higher teachings. The two world-famous epics of India, the *Mahabharata* and the *Ramayana* are included in the Puranas. Both are immensely long—each twice as long as the Bible—and are the popular favorites.

What does *Mahabharata* mean? "Maha" means great and "Bharata" refers to India. Bharata was the ancient name of the first king of India—so it's a story of the great Bharata's descendents, and their wars and struggles with each other.

This semi-historical epic includes many good stories, legends and myths. But in the midst of it, like a jewel embedded in a vast jewel box, occurs the *Bhagavad Gita*. This was one of Shankara's major discoveries. He is the one who singled out this jewel and polished it for Hindus to appreciate, and in due course, the rest of the world.

The *Bhagavad Gita*—featuring Krishna, the most celebrated of avatars, as the central character—is the most popular scripture in India. It is the gospel of Hinduism, more popular than the Upanishads. However, the Upanishads may be considered slightly more prestigious than the *Bhagavad Gita* since they are older and the source of its teachings. In the *Bhagavad Gita* Krishna quotes from the Upanishads to support his own teachings.

The *Ramayana*, which translates as the "Travels of Rama," follows Rama, the prince of Ayodhya, whose wife Sita has been kidnapped by Ravana, the demon king of Lanka. Like the *Bhagavad Gita,* it has many important teachings incorporated within the story.

Rama and Krishna are Christ figures to Hindus. Rama was
Gandhi's ideal. Gandhi's last words as he lay dying were "Rama,
Personal vs.   Rama"—which is interesting, because
Impersonal Worship   Gandhi was chiefly a man of thought
and principles. He was once asked, "Who do you worship?" He
said, "My God is Truth…. There is no god higher than Truth." His
whole life was an attempt to contact the Truth, and to live the Truth.

So Gandhi's God was Truth, and the God of Vedanta is Truth.
But in his meditation Gandhi worshiped Rama. So here is a case
of a man who lived his life very ethically, ascetically, for the purpose of Truth, and yet privately he was a devotional person.
Against the background of the profound philosophical principles
of Vedanta, we find that Gandhi, like other Hindus, and perhaps
like us too, can be devotional as well as philosophical.

We observe that the more advanced Hindus, such as
Shankara and Vivekananda, are typically like that. They are
powerful thinkers, full of mysticism, full of Vedanta, and yet in
their private devotions they are worshipers of some personal form
of the Divine. But not all great teachers are like that; for instance,
Buddha's teachings showed a way to advance spiritually without
any gods or goddesses, since Truth is formless. Buddha urged
worship of the formless Truth.

Buddha's philosophy was very stirring, and many have tried
to follow it. But it's difficult for human beings to follow such an
impersonal path 100 percent of the time. It's helpful to have some
illumined soul, or saint, or incarnation, who you believe was
divine, and who you can turn to when you are not as strong or
philosophical as you would like to be. At those times, Jesus Christ
said, "Come unto me, all ye that labor and are heavy laden, and

I will give you rest." (Matthew 11: 28) So we can turn to Christ or to anyone whom we believe in and who has achieved that state of illumination, who has broken through and is able to help us. Gandhi believed Rama was such a figure.

2

✿ Vedanta and Mysticism

The Vedas, the earliest Hindu scriptures, are a diverse collection of Sanskrit writings concerned with the knowledge of spiritual reality. Vedanta is the philosophy drawn from the Vedas.

Veda means "to know." So the Vedas are works dealing with knowledge. Remembering our definition of Sanskrit as a language meant to express religious thought primarily, this knowledge will be chiefly spiritual or sacred knowledge, not knowledge as we understand it in the West, which is usually scientific, intellectual, or technical knowledge of some kind. The Vedas have other knowledge too, what they call the lower knowledge—that is knowledge of society, crafts, ceremonies, languages—of more ordinary things. But the main idea has always been spiritual knowing. The Vedas are the original, prime, and simple scriptures out of which all the other Hindu scriptures have come.

The early Vedas may have been rendered as far back as 4000 B.C. We are certain that their first mystical traditions started at least three or four thousand years ago. The early writers of the

Vedas, the scribes, were recording a simple relation to the world. There are a lot of tracts about animistic life, descriptions of nature, the sunset, the sunrise, and so on with the gods as major players. This is what we find in all early cultures: They record a sense of the universe with a childlike wonder with their tales, narratives, poetry, and religions. The Vedas have this, too. In addition there are other matters to do with law, marriage, society, food, customs, and various other things. Someone once said that in India if you lose a cow, the Vedas will tell you how to find it.

But gradually, as the centuries passed, around 1500 to 2000 B.C. some of the more sophisticated writers were asking, "Where is this God of the universe that we've heard about? What is this presence we feel in the field and hills, and by the shore?" They began to question, "What is man?" Building on customs, rituals, chants to the sunrise, hymns to Nature, and similar primitive approaches to the universe, they gradually lead to a contemplation of deeper questions: "What is behind all this—this sun, this moon? Why do we exist?" And they began to look within. So gradually the Vedas change their character and become more philosophical. It's a historic moment in world thought when the Vedas turn inward, leading to the conclusions in the Upanishads and the foundation of Vedantic thought.

Vedanta has a threefold definition. Firstly, *ved* is derived from the root *vid*, which means to know in the mystical sense, to know spiritual truth, and *anta* means "end" in the sense of termination, and of purpose. So the first meaning of Vedanta is literally "the scriptures that come at the end of the Vedas." The vast body of religious texts that constitutes the Vedas presents us with themes that are of special interest to Hindus mainly—sacrifices, ancient customs, dietary restrictions, and the like. But at the end is the philosophical section, the Vedanta, the portion known as the Upanishads. This last section was written over a period of about a thousand years, from approximately 1500 B.C. to 500 B.C. The Upanishads themselves grow more sophisticated, subtle, and powerful but always continue with the same themes.

Secondly, the Upanishads are part of the Vedas as the New Testament is part of the Bible. Vedanta is the end, not in the sense of termination but in the sense of the purpose for which the Vedas are written. In other words, the Upanishads are the culmination towards which the Vedas move. The Vedas grow more reflective as they proceed, and become avowedly mystical in the Upanishads.

Finally, Vedanta, the philosophy of the Upanishads, has a third level of interpretation: the *end of knowing*. The Upanishadic sages make the unique, enduring claim that their scriptures represent the summit of all knowledge, the limit of all wisdom. They declare that the penetrating, superconscious insights of the great rishis, corroborating each other's experience over a course of centuries, have enshrined in the Upanishads their realizations with a transparency and comprehensiveness unequalled in any other religious tradition.

So the Upanishads already take this tremendous stand at the very beginning of India's mystical history flourishing in about 1000 B.C., received from the still more ancient Vedas going back into history to an unknown time.

Hinduism has never troubled itself too much about history and dates. In the West we are highly historically oriented and our time consciousness is linear, but this is not the case in India. They don't know the exact dates when their historic figures lived.

The Buddhists and other people have had to tell them when Shankara or Buddha lived. That is their way; Hindus are more concerned with the *now* of things rather than in ancient history. Their feeling is that everything is now, whereas in the West, we feel it happened in the past. According to Muslims, history started with Mohammed's flight from Mecca to Medina; before that, it was a vague ancient history. Christians believe that history began with Jesus; before then was ancient history, but real life began with Christ. Buddhists also believe in Buddha as a great historical figure. So for us who are time-dominated, great things happened once and we still reap the benefits produced by venerable figures such as Moses, Jesus, Mohammed, and Buddha. The majority of the followers of most faiths believe that history begins with their founder. Whereas, the Hindus have a different view, they don't believe that anything began with anyone. They believe that Eternity is now. Everything starts right now; everything is now; nothing began, and nothing ends. It seems that somehow genetically, ethnically, and culturally they have a tendency to believe in the timelessness of things rather than time, and mystics believe this too.

So as we become mystics, we become more like the Hindus in that respect. It's not that we go to India, but we come to re-semble them. To the degree that we are not mystics, to that degree we believe that things happened once, and time and space is our God, that things are real and the world is divided into good and bad, that there's life and death. The Hindus tend to merge every-thing into a universal oneness.

India with its unbroken spiritual tradition is unique as a country. We know that in the ancient world Egypt contributed much to mysticism, with a mystical tradition going back to 1800 to 1500 B.C. Moses of the Jews lived at about this same period. Judaism and other cultures also made their own contributions; for example, the prophets and the mystics of the Old Testament comprised the Jewish mystical tradition. But the Egyptians and the Jews didn't sustain their mystical traditions as a active part of their religions.

The traditional view of God as a being separate from us still dominates the main religions of the West. Although Jewish mysticism has had a revival in modern history in the form of Hasidism and a renewed interest in the Kabbalah, Judaism as a whole is not mystical. It very much believes in this world as reality and a God who is apart and different from the Jews. One of their famous modern philosophers, Martin Buber, describes his God as the "Divine Other." That's also the Muslim view: Allah is above everything, transcending everything, not part of this world. We are working out our destiny while God, separate from all of us, is looking down and judging us. God, as the judge of the Earth, is the Judaic view, the Muslim view, and by and large the Christian view. We don't think that so much now as we used to, thanks to the infusion of Orientalism that has come to our shores over the past century.

In contrast, Hinduism doesn't believe in the separation of things, particularly the individual and God, life and death. Everything flows together.

In the past, the mystic sects of Judaism and Islam, Hasidism and Sufism, respectively, have always had to struggle against a nonmystical dominant majority. But this is not the case in India, where mystics have never been in difficulty. India is the only country in the world where mystics, from the very beginning, were revered and worshiped. In Christianity, mystics have always had to tread a little carefully, as we know. Even though Christianity has produced super figures such as St. Francis of Assisi, St. Teresa of Avila, and Meister Eckhart, they have never really influenced the body of Christianity.

But within Christianity, Judaism, and Islam, some of us have become mystics, or would like to become mystics, and to that **Mysticism**[*] degree we begin to resemble what Hinduism has always had. Somehow we find their thought very sympathetic to us. We begin to think that the present moment is everything and that God is no longer separate from us. We are even questioning a God who is a "He." We could refer to the Supreme as "It," as we do in this text, or "She" for those who find that congenial. Even so, most of us still use "He" because it seems more natural. Of course the nature of the Deity is neither *He* nor is it *She,* It's something else. We have to find out for ourselves as we proceed. But whether we think of it as God, Goddess, or an impersonal force, we have to revere this power behind life. Eventually as mystics or potential mystics we have to have a relationship with this Godhead, this Infinite Source of All. That's the key to the mystic: *A direct personal relationship with this power that is beyond the mind and senses constitutes working mysticism.*

---

[*] Whenever the term *mysticism* is used it does not refer to occult practices, but rather to the doctrine or outlook that declares there is a divine or transcendental reality in the world beyond the mind and the senses. This reality can be contacted and known directly, and everyone has the potential to do this.

So as we become more mystically inclined, we come to resemble the Hindus more and more with their mysticism and their world outlook. We read their scriptures and think, "Well, I've been thinking this way all my life, this is nothing new." We forget the origin of these ideas. It's like the farmer who was taken to see Shakespeare's *Hamlet*. He was an uneducated man, and at the end of the play someone asked him, "How did you like it?"

He replied, "It's all right except for one thing."

"Well, what is that?"

"It was all quotations," he said.

So that is how it is when we read the scriptures. We realize that we've heard these ideas from John Keats or Khalil Gibran or Walt Whitman. They all have these ideas, though they're just quotations: This is where it started. The Upanishads represent the seedbed of everything that is deep, universal, and mystical in the world. So we have a duty to read the Upanishads. There's an old saying in India that a tax should be levied on anyone who has not read the Upanishads. Let us at least be free of that tax.

Philosophically speaking, the dominant mystical idea of the modern world is that the transcendental being and the immanent being that flows through everything are one. Previous to this, it was thought that God or the Supreme Being is transcendental but Other, different. That is still believed officially in the three Western religions, as we've noted. What about the immanent (meaning "dwelling within"), all-pervading spirit that mystics claim? The mystics introduced another kind of Godhead and traditionalists in Christianity, Islam, and Judaism were troubled by it, because the God they worshiped was forever distant, a remote God that you appeased by certain actions, the judge of the earth. But the mystics claim another god, the Godhead, a spirit they uncovered that is not different from their God—a God they worshiped in their own bosom. Slowly these two gods became one and were joined so that these two aspects of the deity are perceived as essentially one. This was the working premise that the Upanishads started with thousands of years ago. These scriptures are unique with their endless emphasis on this central discovery: the Supreme Being is the Self, and your self is that Self.

As we read India's chief scriptures like the Upanishads and the *Bhagavad Gita* we find they are the most sophisticated of all religious writings, as well as the earliest and the most primal. Everything was thought out. Everything was finished before a beginning was made elsewhere. This is what is amazing to us in the West—when we read them we're surprised to find these early works to be so advanced.

We find them so advanced because before the Upanishads were set down, the ancient rishis discovered in themselves a

The Vedantic Principles

transcendental reality beyond the senses, the body, and the intellect, which they realized could not be confined to any one individual. They meditated, analyzed, and reasoned further to conclude that this underlying reality, this Godhead—for they found that It undergirded all other things, and nothing else took precedence over It—must be omnipresent. That is, It must be within everyone, and within every creature. They concluded, therefore, that our real nature is divine. When they conceived of It in an individual sense, the sages called this the *Atman,* or Self—the eternal nature, the Soul. When they equated the Atman with the transcendental reality in its larger, universal sense, they called It *Brahman*. So that the Godhead or Brahman is Atman seen transcendentally, and Atman is Brahman seen in terms of the Soul, the indwelling God.

These insights led the Vedic sages further to proclaim the all-ness of this Brahman or Divine Being: Nothing, they said, exists except the Supreme. Nothing exists outside of It. It creates, pervades, and supports everything. They called It the One. The doctrine of the unity of all existence follows from this.

Thou art That. This aphorism becomes the pinnacle of these daring early conclusions of the Vedic seers whose reasoning was based on their own direct personal experiences.

Given this statement, it becomes obvious, the rishis said, that the aim of life is to unfold and manifest this hidden Godhead, which is present in everyone. Right action is therefore action that unfolds our innate divinity. Wrong action is action that hinders it. The sages did not use the word *sin* as we in the West think of it; they preferred terms such as *ignorance* or *obstacles*.

The goal of life, they said, can be attained by pursuing a path of disciplined and intentional living, with the practice of meditation the chief instrument in this endeavor to remove the obstacles that obstruct the light within.

Vedanta, the sum of what these ancient sages taught, proclaims the universality of Truth, accepting all religions as valid. Different cultures and different faiths abound, but the same divine inspiration exists in all. Ramakrishna, the modern God-man of 19th century India, in his embrace and experience of different religions, verified this truth, which was previously only implicit in Vedanta, that all religions are genuine paths to God-consciousness.

From the beginning the Hindu seers pondered these deep themes. Their complexity was in their religious thought. They dwelled on these concepts endlessly and the result was a highly realized spiritual character unmatched in any other country. To this day the Hindus worship their great yogis and saints, these superhumans who became their exemplars.

So we see the uniqueness of the lives and teachings of these adepts that India has produced by the dozens. Whereas, other religions have matched them only rarely.

If humanity survives for many more millennia, there will be more wings and annexes to that Vedanta edifice—whose main lines remain unchanged since the beginning—since Vedanta by its definition can't be finished because the Truth can never be finished.

3

The Bhagavad Gita

The seminal masterpiece the *Bhagavad Gita* is one of the chief outbuildings of the Vedantic manor house. Although it developed separately from the Vedic tradition, the *Gita* draws its deepest insights from the older scriptures. *Bhagavad Gita,* meaning "Song of the Blessed One," was composed about 500 B.C. The Blessed One is Krishna, one of the great teachers of India. The *Bhagavad*

Gita takes place on a battlefield, one of the numerous battlefields in the *Mahabharata*. Krishna, an incarnation of the Hindu god Vishnu, is the mentor or guru to a famous warrior, Arjuna. Their dialogue, recorded in the *Bhagavad Gita*, consists of Arjuna asking his beloved teacher questions such as: "I don't want to fight, should I fight?" "What is life?" "What is death?" He asks all of the searching questions about life and death and struggle that *we* have asked. Swami Vivekananda, the great modern exponent of Vedantic thought, has described the *Gita* as a bouquet of flowers of spiritual truth drawn from the Upanishads.

The *Bhagavad Gita* can be considered the gospel of Hinduism because it touches on themes such as how to live, how to work, how to relate to family, how to bring up children, the problem of work, the problem of sex, and the social structure. Hinduism as a whole is presented beautifully in the *Bhagavad Gita*, better than in the Upanishads, which have a different focus and therefore don't apply themselves to these everyday concerns. More so than any other scripture, the *Bhagavad Gita* shows us how to live in the world while leading a spiritual life. There is something in it for each psychological type and spiritual need.

The key word in the *Bhagavad Gita* is *yoga*.[1] One meaning of yoga is "yoke" or "joining together." Here it refers to joining with God, so that the four main disciplines or

The Four Yogas

yogas in Hinduism that lead to union with God are *bhakti* yoga, *karma* yoga, *raja* yoga and *jnana* yoga. Bhakti yoga is the yoga of devotion, in which one cultivates love for a divine incarnation or personal aspect of the Divine through worship, prayer, and *japa* or *japam* (the repetition of a mantram or divine name). It is suited to spiritual aspirants with a devotional nature who prefer having a personal relationship with God in one of the various modes such as servant, child, lover, parent, or friend of the Deity. Bhakti yoga is the simplest and easiest path to follow, especially for those of us who are inclined this way. Most followers of all the major religions are practitioners of this path.

Karma yoga is the yoga of work or selfless action. Action performed in this way is truly yoga in practice. It is suited to those with active natures. More on this path will follow.

Raja yoga, the yoga of meditation and concentration, is for those who are mystically inclined. The goal is to still the mind through the practice of meditation so that the true nature of the Self, which is pure, perfect, and immortal, is realized.

Jnana yoga is the yoga of the knowledge of Brahman for those intellectually inclined. It is the path of self-analysis, discrimination, and complete renunciation. *"Neti neti,"* or "not this, not this" is the saying that characterizes the discrimination required to discern the real from the unreal. It is the most difficult path. The *Katha Upanishad* compares this path to a razor's edge.

The *Bhagavad Gita* deals with all four yogas, but particularly with karma yoga.

DHARMA

In the *Gita* Krishna represents the higher self, the spiritual consciousness, addressing the ordinary, confused self—in this case, the warrior Arjuna, one of the Pandava brothers, who faces the greatest crisis in his experience.

Arjuna is confronted with having to fight and kill those who have joined the army of his evil cousin Duryodhana, who has deprived Arjuna and his brothers of their rightful kingdom. Among the forces opposing the Pandava brothers are their teachers, estranged close relatives and friends. Duryodhana's armies are formidable and far outnumber those of the Pandava brothers, but the brothers are great warriors and have Krishna on their side. Krishna becomes the charioteer for Arjuna to help guide him along the right path.

Hitherto Arjuna has been an exemplary functionary, a trained, pious, faithful, efficient, confident, and orthodox servant of society. But now his values fail him—values that he had *received* as inherently true. Now he has to discover another set of values within himself. He has to become a yogi, a mystic, a man of self-realization.

In his crisis, Arjuna, the noble warrior, suddenly becomes a pacifist. "Resist not evil" is his cry. But he sees the evil, and he knows that he must resist it—especially since as a warrior it is his special duty or *dharma* to do so. Dharma means literally "that which holds together." Its primary meaning is "the inmost constitution of the thing, the law of its inner being." The secondary meaning is religion, righteousness, duty. A man's dharma is created by his own past actions. Arjuna was born a warrior; therefore his dharma is to fight.

There is immense significance in Krishna's instructions to Arjuna on the true nature of action, and the true method of acting.

Karma Yoga Great stress, then, is placed on karma yoga in the *Gita*. Karma yoga is action performed with spiritual rather than selfish motives. It is working without thought of gain. One immediate advantage of karma yoga is that every unselfish action brings its own spiritual realization. Through this path one gains purity of heart.

So karma yoga illuminates the whole spiritual path. Are we bound? Are we in a state of bondage? This yoga teaches us very quickly *how* bound we actually are. It is a blessing to discover so vital a truth about our condition.

Arjuna's hesitation on the battlefield of life is due to ignorance of the Truth, that is to say, ignorance of his own nature and the nature of humanity. Growth in wisdom and enlightenment will strengthen him and free him from his crisis.

So we see that Krishna's summons to Arjuna is to "Know this Atman," to realize the Truth within. His description of the Atman is an evocation of the Soul, the Self—within Arjuna himself.

Krishna tells Arjuna:

That which is nonexistent can never come into being, and that which is can never cease to be. Those who have known the inmost Reality know also the nature of is and is not.

That Reality which pervades the universe is indestructible. No one has power to change the Changeless.

Bodies are said to die, but That which possesses the body is eternal. It cannot be limited, or destroyed. Therefore you must fight....

> Know this Atman...
> Unchanging for ever.
> How can It die
> The death of the body?...
>
> Dream not you do
> The deed of the killer,

> Dream not the power
> Is yours to command it....

The Atman cannot be manifested to the senses, or thought about by the mind. It is not subject to modification. Since you know this, you should not grieve.[2]

For those who are not yet ready for the higher teachings of the Upanishads, the *Gita* provides a compromise. Krishna says,

The Avatar as Savior

in effect, "If these ideas are too much for you, Arjuna—you the warrior, you my student who represents Everyman—then throw the burden on me. If you can't live up to these truths of the scriptures, if Truth is too strong for you, if you don't know what the Self means, if you don't know what Brahman means, if you can't follow such an austere path, Arjuna, then throw all the burden on me. I will save you. Worship me and I will carry you across this ocean of worldliness to the other shore." But this is not Krishna's first recommendation. In the early chapters of the *Gita* he says, "Be illumined, Arjuna. Be a yogi, be a knower of the Truth. Stand up and know what the Self is, what you are." In other words, stand on the strength of the Atman within you— that is your nature. But Arjuna says, "Sometimes I get so tired. I get confused. I can't control my mind." When we are weary and heavy laden, tired or confused, that is when Jesus or Krishna is very helpful. "If that is the case," says Krishna, or Jesus, "all right, then worship me, and throw the burden on me. I will carry you across."

It isn't so easy though, to give everything to a Christ or a Krishna. It's easy to say, but harder to do. We have to be almost as dedicated as the knower of the Truth is. But it is still a kind of compromise. It makes us understand that human nature cannot always stand the strain of these deep ideas, the mysticism of Vedanta and the Upanishads. We yearn for something closer and more concrete than that. In that case Christ is there, or Buddha, or Krishna, or the saints—women and men, great figures—or whoever we may worship as an incarnation, as an embodiment of these ideas.

Sri Krishna, in the *Gita,* is regarded as a full manifestation of the Absolute. As such, he is able to explain such profound matters as what this world is and what Nature is; what man is; what the nature of ultimate reality is and what the relation is between these three, the world, man, and ultimate reality.

Krishna's greatest significance in the largest sense is as a speaker of Truth in the *Bhagavad Gita* and a commentator on Vedanta, and the Upanishads, but even he cannot absorb Hinduism: Hinduism is larger than Krishna or anyone else. Whereas, we find that Jesus absorbs Christianity. That is a wonderful thing in a way, but it's risky when everything is identified with one man's life. Supposing it was proven that Christ never lived, or that Mohammed, the founder of Islam, or Buddha the founder of Buddhism, never lived, then those religions would have no foundation. This is very unlikely, but you can imagine the tremendous problem it would pose. It's interesting to speculate on the rationale of India's feeling that law and principle are higher than any individual. Even their eminent figures such as Rama and Krishna, who are revered as highly as Christ is revered in the West, are not large enough to stand for Hinduism.

Hinduism is a system of spiritual laws that are believed to be eternal—they have always existed and always will exist. And since Truth always will exist, it can never be enclosed; it can never be finished. Each new century discovers something that past centuries have not discovered. For instance, Swami Vivekananda (1863–1902), rivals Shankara for depth of insight in interpreting the Upanishads and the Vedanta philosophy. Vivekananda is not the last such interpreter; there will be still others. That manor house is not yet completed.

4

 # Yoga

The Yoga system is another of Hinduism's six schools of philosophy. Yoga is a way—formulated and codified—that the Hindu mystic, or anyone interested in the philosophical principles revealed in the Upanishads, tries to implement these principles. It is a means of attaining, by practice and self-control, the transcendental experiences reported in the Upanishads. It is the soul seeking knowledge and experience of itself.

Therefore, when we use the term *yoga,* we won't be referring to *hatha yoga* exercises but the other field—the yoga of meditation, the yoga system linked to the Upanishads. In
Hatha Yoga
the West the word *yoga* is used loosely for many things, including a regimen of well-known physical exercises (or *asanas)* called hatha yoga, which is merely one of its limbs.

In fact, these asanas are essentially a spiritual approach to physical exercise and the body, aimed at psychological well-being as much as physical values such as self-control, inner poise, self-knowledge, and self-awareness. But more importantly, the concept of yoga encompasses raja yoga, the practice of meditation, mental analysis, and concentration. This is described in detail by Patanjali in his *Yoga Aphorisms,* also known as the *Yoga Sutras. Sutra* means a thread, so it refers to the yoga scriptures that are like threads—bare, succinct statements of the Truth with beads of commentary placed on them.

The Upanishadic sages developed yoga philosophy long before Patanjali,[3] who was a contemporary with Christ. This

Patanjali, Yoga's Codifier

philosophy was orally transmitted very faithfully from teacher to student for centuries before Patanjali, the great legendary yogi, captured the verbal yoga tradition and put forth in writing for the first time the psychology of yoga. In this distinctive system of thought the law of subjectivity is discovered and promulgated, and the inner path is made a matter of scientific law.

In addition, Patanjali was the first to enthrone meditation in all its complex glory. We read in the Upanishads, "By meditation realize the truth. He is realized by meditation and truthfulness." The Upanishads state this but don't discuss it; Patanjali discussed it in detail.

MEDITATION

In the *Yoga Aphorisms* meditation is discovered and presented as the means to realizing the light within, the Self within. By meditation we chiefly mean yoga, and it is the heart of yoga, although yoga is more than meditation; it has an ethical and moral background as well. The first steps in this system focus on the development of character. A moral and ethical foundation needs to be established before one is fit for the practice of meditation and concentration. But essentially for our purposes here, meditation is yoga's chief thrust and practice by which the Self is realized.

One of the all-time great achievements was by Patanjali when he discovered that whatever served to advance meditation was good and whatever did not advance meditation was evil. A way of life that advances meditation and the meditative state is good, is an absolute right. And anything that does not advance it, that tends to hobble it—a way of life, or attitude, or activity, or value, or book or whatever—is an evil. This is the yardstick: whatever makes the mind calm, that's good. Whatever makes the mind restless, that's evil. Patanjali saw clearly that in order to realize the Deity, the Truth within, we have to do it through meditation. Prayer and good works are helpful, though they haven't brought us too far—mainly because we haven't learned how to do them in the right spirit. They are appendages to spiritual life and we have to go through them, but they lack a central yardstick, a central principle to which everything is related. That is meditation, and naturally, that means the mind. The mind is going to be affected by meditation.

According to this practice, we can realize the Truth only through meditation; therefore, we have to learn to meditate. There are certain ways to meditate that are right, and certain ways that are not right. We have to find out the right way. Making the mind a blank is not a good way. We may have read that in a book: Make the mind a blank. Before we listen to anyone in such an important area, we should find out their credentials. Or someone else may say, well, meditation is just relaxation. These relaxation therapies have value. They enable us to cope better in the stressful world we live in. Anything that can contribute to our peace of mind is of value, *but* they don't lead us to the Truth.

When we have learned the right way to meditate, we find that certain conditions, including a certain state of mind, are necessary to meditate well. Other states of mind are inimical to meditation. Therefore, what will help the mind to be calm and collected is what we want. Patanjali sees this in a flash. Of course this was known in the Upanishads. Calmness, tranquility, serenity—those words occur all through the Upanishads; they are self-evident to the sages. But Patanjali says that it's not self-evident, that it needs to be spelled out for those who are not sages, but who want to become sages through the ladder of ethical development. So that is what he did.

We see that we have to be calm to meditate. We can't meditate when we're restless. When we're restless, instead of meditating we should pray, or repeat a mantram, take a walk, take a cold shower, do hatha yoga exercises or other things, because meditation at this time will make things worse. Unless we're calm, meditation will only intensify the cause of the restlessness. So we don't meditate when we're restless, only when we're calm. Therefore whatever makes us calm or keeps us calm is good: Our mind will be in a state to meditate and through meditation our mind will get closer to the Truth. Therefore calmness is indispensable on the way to the Truth. Whatever gives us a feeling of peace and calm is an absolute good. It's part of the universal morality, the subjective fact we all discover.

If we had to pinpoint what India's great discovery is, it is meditation itself, which makes realization and mysticism possible. Without a systematic approach to working with the mind, we have a series of thoughts and brilliant speculations, such as we might find at universities, but nothing real. Like when we take courses in philosophy at a university, it's stimulating. It's rather interesting in many ways to read the leading authors and thinkers, but it doesn't seem real because, to begin with, they all differ from one another. Kant differs from Spinoza. Plato differs from Aristotle. Who is right? You go to the professor and he says, well, it depends. He doesn't know himself what the truth is. The twelve great philosophers of the West all differ from each other. At the end of the course we are only more confused than we were at the beginning.

According to Vedanta, Truth is absolute. It's eternal and universal. So those courses, writers, and philosophers are inadequate. They are working in another vein—brilliantly and very persuasively—with a limited section of the mind, a more surface vein of the mind called the intellect. They are not working within the mystical center, what we might call the intuitive center—intuition perfected. So how does this intuitive center open up? Through meditation and spiritual disciplines. Those Western philosophers didn't meditate; they were mere intellectuals. If you go to the professors of philosophy at the university and ask them, "Do you meditate?" They will likely say, "No, we haven't found that to be necessary," or something like that. They think that the intellect is enough. Not so, the intellect is shallow in terms of the total mind. Though brilliant and necessary as intellect is, it's still a surface instrument. The yogi or the saint awakens and uncovers depths unknown. Even those of us who meditate and who are not saints discover something of the same thing—intuitive powers dawn within us and we begin to be guided by them. We begin to see what Patanjali achieved with his discovery of meditation—which was unknown to the ancient cultures of Greece, Rome, Egypt, Israel, and China, although there are always individuals here and there that discover it, but not with the same methodical approach that we find in India.

In its systematic approach, yoga treats the mind as an organ of perception, a receiver of light, an instrument of spiritual development—not as a source of light itself.

**The Mind,
An Instrument**

The mind is simply to be brought into a state of sustained concentration, inward intro-spection, and purified absorption in its own inner being, beyond the emotional and psychological centers that lie close to the mind's surface. In this collected, stilled, and focused state the mind becomes a magnifying lens capable of concentrating to a point the previously and characteristically scattered rays of itself, as a magnifying lens concentrates the scattered rays of the sun. Then the Self illuminates the purified, still, and collected mind with its own presence in a blaze of divine light. This breakthrough experi-ence is referred to as *samadhi,* of which there are many different levels. Patanjali defines it as a state of yoga or union in which the true essence of the object shines forth, without any distortion by the mind of the perceiver. The treasure is already present within;

through meditative practices the mind is used as an instrument with which to seek it.

The word *yoga* also refers to the state attained by union of what was previously felt to be two: the individual mind and the Universal Mind, the individual soul and the Universal Soul or Self; or, in Christian terms, the Soul and God.

Therefore, in purely Vedantic terms the Self can be known by direct experience. One becomes by *realization* what one was before in potential—the Divine Self. The practice of yoga can provide the foundation for this illumination.

Next, we turn to the Upanishads, which represent the manor house itself of Vedanta.

PART TWO

The Upanishads:
Thou Art That

Vedanta is rooted in the supreme scriptures of India, the Upanishads, which culminate the Hindu sacred writings known as the Vedas. Some background on these incomparable scriptures will be helpful. Varying in length from two verses to two hundred, there are approximately one hundred individual Upanishads, of which ten or eleven are considered major. They are sometimes named after the sage who is a leading speaker in the dialogue or the treatise. This is true of the *Swetasvatara Upanishad,* from which we shall largely quote.

In the Upanishads it is as though the sages can't recover from the wonder of their revelation of the truth about the identity and oneness of the Divine with the individual. Every part is permeated with the excitement of their discovery. This gives the Upanishads their unique charm.

To some degree the Vedic seers speak about how we are to realize the truth, but for the most part they hope simply to draw us towards realization through logic, intuition, illustration, poetry, philosophical discrimination, and dialogue. In other words, they use every possible means in their attempt to turn the mind away from its ordinary outward tendencies toward the world around us and to dramatically mesmerize it, so to speak, with the thought that our true nature is divine. We see this in the Upanishads; then with the *Bhagavad Gita* we find out how we are to live.

5

ꙮ The Swetasvatara Upanishad

The *Swetasvatara Upanishad* is a concentrated and detailed work that distills most of the vital thought of earlier Upanishads while, at the same time, making its own inimitable contribution—as each Upanishad does—to the rich tapestry of Vedantic philosophy.

"What is that, by knowing which, all other things may be known?" That is the basic question of the Upanishads. In one way or another each one endlessly works changes on that theme: "What is the cause of this universe? ... Whence do we come? ... Why do we live?"[4] The *Swetasvatara* and other Upanishads begin in this simple, almost innocent way. They inquire about the cause: "Time, space, law, chance, matter, energy, intelligence...." Is it all chance? Is it all a blind fortuitous conflict of atoms? Is it energy? Is it mind? We are still asking ourselves these very questions.

The Upanishads conclude—sometimes cryptically, sometimes after developing the idea at length—that none of these possibilities can be the cause. They are all effects—creations of mind in some cases, of the cosmic will in others. Time and space are adjuncts of the human mind; they have no essential reality in themselves. It is equally obvious that matter or chance cannot be the cause.

What about energy? We hear much about this today. Electronics is today's theme. At one time a computer company

37

had a very effective advertisement that showed a picture of energy

Energy   visualized, with the caption: "Think of the com-
                    puter as energy—mental energy." Some people
identify energy with the Godhead itself because that is how we
think in this age. It is a step forward, certainly. Two hundred years
ago people regarded the Deity as a grand machine. This was the
age of Newtonian physics, which presented an essentially
mechanistic view of the universe, added to which was the dawn
of the Industrial Revolution, the Machine Age. People were
influenced intellectually by Newton's conception of the world,
and society itself developed corresponding views of the 'good
life'. "God is like that too," they said. The result was a mechanical
God that created the world and then stepped aside to watch it run
perfectly like clockwork, without doing anything more about it.

Today, in the midst of a world focused on energy, we have
made a big advance over that view, but perhaps not the final
advance. We have yet, for instance, to reach the point where we
think of things in terms of mind and live in a mental world. Some
individuals have, though, and when greater and greater numbers
of people begin to think in those terms, we'll have the Deity as
Mind—yet even that is not the ultimate goal.

Energy cannot be the cause because the first thing we are
aware of when we search for the origin of things is something
like ourselves, a knowing entity, a conscious being. Energy is
nonconscious. The nonconscious cannot be the cause of the
conscious. This is the way the sages reason in the Upanishads.
Matter cannot be the cause, for the same reason. And mind
(intelligence they equate with mental activity) cannot be the cause
because it is changeable, fluctuating constantly. The rishis go

deeper than matter, than energy, than mind. Notice the gradation: matter—energy—mind.

"They are effects and exist to serve the soul."[5] This is the view of Vedanta: the whole universe exists ultimately to serve the soul, to give it self-knowledge.

The soul is *entombed* in the body. Thus, it forgets its origin and true nature and gradually loses all sense of its own reality. So that when we say *self-knowledge* we really mean *soul*-knowledge, the soul coming into knowledge of its own divinity.

It is the Vedantic view that the human soul, the Self, the Atman, is identical with Brahman, the Godhead. In fact, the soul's experience in mystical realization is the ecstasy of discovering its oneness with that from which it had thought itself so distant. That is the ineffable experience, according to Vedanta. The sages found the One, the Godhead, the transcendental reality called Brahman, dwelling within, indivisible—neither existence nor nonexistence—something indescribable.

ONE WITHOUT A SECOND

> The seers, absorbed in contemplation, saw within themselves the ultimate reality, the self-luminous being, the one God, who dwells as the self-conscious power in all creatures. He is One without a second.[6]

One without a second—This phrase would serve as the whole of the Upanishads if we could read in it deeply enough. We have endless food for reflection in this single thought.

One without a second. There is only one—Brahman alone in his glory, in his majesty, in his uniqueness. He is the creator of everything, the encloser of everything. The Upanishads say not only that, but that He is the existence of everything—He is existence absolute, which is the first description of the Supreme.

That means not only does this Ultimate Reality exist: It *is* existence, so we partake of that same existence. We may have many differences between us, yet the one thing we all have in common is that each of us draws from the same hidden power within us. Again, the Upanishads say that this 'otherness' of the Deity is only a mirage. It's hard to separate oneself from one's own existence.

In Hinduism, Brahman has three irreducible attributes. He is *Sat-Chid-Ananda:* existence absolute, knowledge absolute, and bliss absolute. This theme is reflected throughout the Upanishads. The Supreme is pure existence, pure knowledge or, as Buddha might say, pure truth, and It is also pure bliss or pure love.

Whereas we think love as we know it is the highest thing, the Hindus say that although love is very high, it's a lower form of bliss; bliss is higher. How can they say that? The love that we know or feel or project is always mixed with our personalities as they are at any given moment. So the love that we project or experience unfortunately is never pure, is never the essential thing. In our best moments love may be particularly strong and pure, but those moments are rare—and they are usually moments when we are alone.

Even in its mixed form, love is still one of the most wonderful things we have. What would it be in its unmixed form? That's what the mystic wants; he or she wants the unmixed essence only. So the mystic turns away from the many faces of love and seeks Love Itself within.

The rishis in particular were powerful examiners, extreme analysts of everything to do with religion. They accepted this and other ideas that were later set down in the scriptures as being true to their experience—not only true of the Deity but true of themselves as well. How can they postulate a description of the Deity, which is unknown by most of us, unless they had a close relationship with and intimate knowledge of It? Where did they get that from? From their own experiences of the Divine.

These sages discovered the nature of the Deity by discovering the nature of the human being first. First man, then God. That is why they have this intimate way of talking about the Deity. They start with man and then they find God in man, but man in his true essence.

FORCES THAT MOVE US: THE GUNAS

> Deep within all beings the [Ultimate Reality] dwells, hidden from sight by the coverings of the gunas—sattwa, rajas, and tamas. He presides over time, space and all apparent causes.[7]

Early in the *Swetasvatara Upanishad* the three *gunas* appear— *sattwa or sattva, rajas,* and *tamas. Gunas* means "fetters" and, by extension, the elements that compose matter and the forces that drive *through* matter. The gunas are what constitute the universe of mind and matter. They are the impulses that propel us onward or backward. They are also the *moods* that possess us and push us into certain actions and conditions. We think *we* are responsible, but the gunas are: We are under their control.

Tamas is a condition of indolence, darkness, laziness and delusion. In the tamasic state we manifest dullness and lethargy. **Tamas** We are led to do certain things, eat particular foods, seek out others agreeable to this condition. We have all known this state; and some are plunged in tamas their whole lifetime. According to Vedanta, these tamasic individuals do not yet know what moral life is—they must pass through this guna first. But even individuals on a higher plane occasionally fall into tamas.

Rajas Rajas is the mood of activity, energy, will, ambition— sometimes in a good sense, such as getting an education or raising a family, objectives for which you need a lot of energy. If we are immersed in tamas and these challenges confront us, we don't feel like dealing with them; nothing is worthwhile. We have to use rajas to conquer tamas. In that sense rajas is a good thing. But it is also a potential liability; it has to be watched. Rajas can become mere self-assertion, blind driving energy, an egoistic approach to life. If left alone and unchecked, rajas becomes almost as dangerous as tamas. If guided by the enlightened will, rajas can be used for our higher purpose—it propels us forward.

Sattva Sattva is still higher than rajas. This is the quality of spiritual knowledge, the tranquil mood, the serene guna in which we seem to be at peace with everyone. Although sattva has an outward resemblance to tamas, it is quite the opposite of indolence. The serene and detached person may seem lethargic because he or she is not caught up in activity. Yet sattva is still a condition, an element, an energy that we attain when we work hard to overcome tamas with the help of rajas, and rajas with the help of sattva. With sattva dominant, we are in a position to go beyond the gunas and move on to spiritual truth.

We cannot know truth in the midst of the two lower gunas. In rajas we are caught in the coils of forces both good and bad, and we cannot see things clearly enough. The clear-sightedness we seek is the unique advantage of meditation, by which—even if we are a rajasic personality type—we can cultivate willed moments of sattva. We can be full of distractions and turmoil, yet train ourselves to sit still, collect our mind, induce a sattvic mood of tranquility, and enter into a contemplative state.

Nonetheless, sattva is still a guna. We can see how tamas and rajas are bonds that absorb and imprison us when we are under their control, but how can sattva also be bondage? Those who are of a sattvic temperament are admirable and true, with their calm personalities and graceful relationships, their love of art, music, literature, and philosophy—but they rarely seek God. The very richness of their lives displaces the hunger for God. You hardly ever find a refined person, distinguished for their intellect, education, and graceful manners, who is also a passionate seeker for God. Why should this be? Because sattva is a guna: It's a gentle trap, a silken cord, but a powerful one just the same. It's hard to exhaust the richness of a sattvic person's life. Such a person doesn't feel they need God when he or she has everything else. We go to God when there is a need, a gnawing hunger—that's when we seek God. How can we produce that? We can't. Without that hunger these are just wonderful ideas. Unless you are hungry, food doesn't mean anything to you.

So sattva is a guna, even though we tend to think that sattvic people are close to God. In the Upanishads there's no explanation of this, it's just put forth as obvious—it's assumed that the initiate would know that sattva is also bondage.

There is an ancient story related to this. A man is passing through a forest when three robbers attack him. They fall upon him, knock him down, and take all his possessions. Then one of the robbers says, "Let's kill him." The second robber replies, "No, why kill him? We'll tie him up." So they tie him up and leave. Meanwhile, as the man is lying there, the third robber creeps back and removes the man's bonds, tends his wounds, and shows him the way out of the forest. The man is so grateful that he says, "Come with me to my house." But the robber responds, "No, I'm sorry; I'll get arrested. You must go alone, but I can point the way."

The forest represents life, though it could also represent the forest of the mind, which is always implied in these Hindu allegories. In this parable we are attacked by the gunas, the three robbers. Tamas is the first robber, who wants to kill us. Rajas is the second robber, who wants to bind us tightly to the world with his fierce energy and ferocity, leaving us confused and bewildered. The third robber, sattva, removes the bonds and binds up the wounds that have been inflicted by his companions. Sattva comforts us, enlightens us, and shows us the way out. Finally when ready to leave, we're very grateful to sattva, forgetting that he was one of the original robbers. We say to sattva, "Come with me." But he can't: Sattva points the way to the soul, to the Self, to the Truth, but once having seen us on our way, he rejoins his two companions.

These gunas, these forces, these tendencies within us, keep us from seeing the light in others and the light in ourselves. There

The Clouds of The Soul

is a constant play in our lives between them and their endless combinations. Sometimes we're in thrall of one, two or all three gunas, oscillating from one to the other. And each one of these moods, these gunas, seem real at the time, yet they are no more real than the passage of clouds before the sun.

In this analogy, the clouds are not real; the sun is real. Similarly, rain and snow seem real, but they have a temporary reality — they pass and then where are they? They're gone. Where is their reality? Meanwhile, the sun hidden behind the storm clouds is steady all the time — *that* is the real. So you have the Self within you, the light, always burning, always there. Passing in front of it are the gunas, the weather conditions of your mind, of your personality. These conditions appear and make you forget the sun, and instead make you aware only of the snow, the hail, the sleet, the rain, and the darkness. All we are aware of is the changing weather caused by these gunas, these weather conditions of the soul.

Someone asks us, "Do you believe in the soul?" We may think we believe in the soul but in fact we believe in the weather more than the soul. These weather conditions worry us and occupy most of our mental time and energy. The sun is always the same; its nature is changelessness, as St. Paul says, the same yesterday, today, and forever. The sun is like that, and the Self is like that.

We can think of the gunas as moods, as powerful, gripping vises, sometimes seizing us for days. These forces are not only powerful in themselves, but have the power to persuade us that they are real. But Brahman is like the sun presiding over all: "He presides over time, space, and all apparent causes."

The sun and not the clouds that cover it is the cause of our world, producing heat, energy, and light. We worry about the weather, "What will it be like today? Will it be overcast or bring rain, or sleet?" Meanwhile, the sun is there, serene, presiding over everything. The weather report for the sun is always bright, immortal, unchanging. Although we know it's always the same, the difficulty is that we can't always see it, or find it. If we could find it, we would know that it's unchanging. No weather report is needed.

These gunas, then, are the forces that move us through life.

THE WHEEL OF KARMA

We read in the *Swetasvatara Upanishad:*

> This vast universe is a wheel. Upon it are all creatures that are subject to birth, death, and rebirth. Round and round it turns, and never stops. It is the wheel of Brahman. As long as the individual self thinks it is separate from Brahman, it revolves upon the wheel in bondage to the laws of birth, death, and rebirth. But when through the grace of Brahman it realizes its identity with him, it revolves upon the wheel no longer. It achieves immortality.[8]

Karma refers to the law of cause and effect. As we know from physics, every action produces an effect. A person's karma is the sum total of all the results of his or her actions in this and in previous lifetimes. The wheel of karma, of endless becoming or reincarnation here is called the wheel of Brahman. We get on that wheel and never get off—unless, according to Vedantists, we come to know the Self, the Truth of Brahman.

There is an important hiatus in the midst of the significant sentence: "As long as the individual self thinks it is separate from Brahman, it revolves upon the wheel in bondage to the laws of birth, death, and rebirth." What actually brings about the revolving upon the wheel is not immediately apparent. "The individual self thinks it is separate from Brahman" — isn't this in itself that which causes the wheel of bondage to revolve? Not precisely. There is a missing link between the two parts of the sentence, and that is the phenomenon of desire. This, in fact, is assumed in the text. It is desire that causes the wheel to revolve, and the bondage to grow.

The moment we think we are separate from Brahman, or separate from anything in this world, trouble starts. We begin to generate a false conception of ourselves and of life almost immediately. The forgetting of our oneness with Brahman, then, is not in itself the precise cause of the turning of this wheel and the increasing of our bondage, but rather that which inevitably *results* in the interval between the two: the arising of desire. And desire comes from forgetting the Truth. Notice the sequence of thought: We desire something because of a feeling of need and insufficiency. This feeling of want is itself created by our forgetfulness of who we are, forgetfulness of Reality, of our oneness with Brahman. Desire, then, is the dynamic power that causes the wheel to turn and bondage to grow.

When we remember God we cease to desire. The wheel stops turning. Forgetting the Divine produces a feeling of need, and then desire and anxiety arise. This was Buddha's tragic discovery. Under the bodhi tree he saw the world of humanity caught on a huge wheel, unable to get off. It was desire, ignorance, craving that kept them on the wheel birth after birth, from which there was no escape ... until we know Truth directly, then only can we break this knot of karma and achieve *Being*.

Becoming is eternal, without end. Being is something beyond: When known at a certain stage, it frees us from the fatal chain of moral causation. That is, we sow a thought, reap an action; sow an action, reap a habit; sow a habit, reap a character; sow a character, reap a destiny—we are thus caught up in this endless round. We must do it all *knowingly:* We must consciously sow thoughts to reap intentional actions, to reap premeditated habits—and another destiny.

BRAHMAN: THE ABSOLUTE

Brahman is the Godhead in Vedanta philosophy, the impersonal Absolute that has become the world.

This Brahman can't be located in one place in the universe, since It is indivisible. It is the support of the heavens and of all the worlds. It is Spirit, but It is also Energy; It is Mind, and something unknowable. It has its locus in the human heart—indeed, It exists everywhere. It can only be known, however, in a higher form of life—Its divinity sleeps in the stone and the plant, stirs in the animal, wakes in the human, and knows Itself in the awakened soul. In each evolving form of this hierarchy of consciousness, the Absolute Existence has more and more opportunity to know Itself. In fact, this is the only way It does know itself—through the mirroring soul of the saint. For It is the Eternal Knower, the Eternal Subject—It cannot be an object of anybody's knowledge. It is through the reflecting mirror of that awakened soul that It becomes known to Itself.

> The truth is that you are always united with the Lord but you must know this. Nothing further is there to know.[9]

We feel separate from the Supreme, but we are one with It. We must realize this truth. Vedanta says that this Indivisible

Reality has become everything and filled everything. Humanity is one with It and therefore is also divine. The purpose of life is to realize that divinity.

Vedanta accepts each religion as inspired because each is pervaded by Brahman. Vedanta also accepts all the divine incarnations and major prophets as inspired; they are the messengers of Brahman.

Buddha had an experience of It—the Unutterable—and chose not to talk about what he had encountered. There are two possible reactions after an experience of the Supreme. One is to do what the Upanishads attempt: try to communicate to those who have not had the experience, in such a dazzling and tireless way that we feel that there *must* be something there and we are led to try for it ourselves. The other response is to say nothing: the experience is inexpressible. Such an experience is beyond the comprehension of those who have not had it. Buddha refused to talk about what he had experienced, deciding instead to discuss things we can understand. His was a different approach to the same reality, and both are valid.

There can't be two ultimates. We are looking for *the* Ultimate, and one personality experiencing It may have a different interpretation from another. A very devotional type of person may be driven to sing the glories of Brahman endlessly as the *Swetasvatara Upanishad* does: "I have known beyond all darkness that great Person of Golden Effulgence... He is the great Light shining forever."[10] A more austere mind—imperturbable, analytical—will perceive the Light in another dimension and will announce It differently.

The Supreme is like the light that comes through the prism

in a window. The prism is turned one way, and it is a white light; another way, and it is a blue light; a third way, and we find still another color. But chiefly we want to know—*is there a Light there to begin with?* And the Upanishadic sages affirm that there is. But depending on the culture, the prophet, the age, and on many other things, the Light coming through will be described in various terms.

If someone told us that there is fire in a handful of sticks that a boy is holding, the ordinary mind would deny the report of the senses, seeing no fire, only sticks. What you declare, we would think, is a kind of delusion. This is the approach of the everyday creature-mind to someone who says that Brahman is within:

> Fire, though present in the firesticks, is not perceived until one stick is rubbed against another. The Self is like that fire: It is realized in the body by meditation on the sacred syllable OM.[11]

We've heard much about the syllable OM. Its Sanskrit symbol, ॐ, is becoming increasingly visible in modern times. Originally the syllable was spelled AUM—and that ॐ **OM** remains the proper spelling today. But when it is pronounced steadily in a chanting intonation, it becomes more like OM. The three letters—A, U, and M—are said to represent the types of sounds that the human throat can make: *A* is the least differentiated sound, *U* the middle differentiated sound, and *M* the most differentiated.

When we try to think of God or the Divine Being, we have only the mind to think with. The mind is our instrument, our creature; before we can succeed, we have to find out what its nature is. Among other things, our mind lives for sense impressions, concrete realities. That is what makes it comfortable. If you give it a concept like Immortality, it grows restless and uneasy. Give it Love, and it is restless even there: It tries to think of love and immediately turns to a sense object, something specific. We tell it to think of Glory and it can't—it again identifies with the familiar.

So it's clear that if you want to think of anything—not only these abstractions but anything at all—you need a name or a word to think with. That is the mind's nature. We have to give it a word or a name before it can have a thought; it needs to know what to think to begin with, and to be able to think. Every thought in the world has a corresponding word or name that announces it to the mind.

When we want to think of God, the mind wanders in a void. It thinks of the sky perhaps, but even that is something definite— blue, somewhat tangible. We need a name for God, or a word. We can't think of the Absolute itself: we need something to give the mind some support to hold onto. As we have seen, if you tell the mind to think of Love, it gets restless, but if you think of some aspect of Love or some loving person—an image or symbol— immediately it feels more comfortable. Therefore we give it what it needs.

There are many visual symbols for the Divine. Christ is one; he is a vehicle towards Brahman, a channel towards the Absolute. He did not point to himself, but beyond. Buddha, also, said, Don't glorify *me;* tread the path that I have trodden, and you can experience what I have.

With OM we're concerned with another kind of symbol, the auditory. It is the one sound-symbol that has persisted for millennia. It is such an ancient sound that it is almost certain Buddha himself used it in his spiritual exercises; it was already old by that time. Very likely Christ used it too. Throughout the time of Christ, and until 300 or 400 A.D., through the age of Plotinus and after—India's mystical tradition had continued with marked influence. As a great vortex of spirituality, India was calling many Westerners and Near Easterners to drink at her mystic springs. It is even rumored that during the twelve unknown years of Christ, he went to India—a hermetic tradition has always testified to this. Plato is also said to have gone there. Plotinus, one of the major Western mystics, wanted to go there. Thus it is very possible that Christ himself discovered this sound, at least would have heard of it during his years of development. It is certain that Buddha, raised a Hindu and for a long time a practitioner of traditional disciplines, would have used it as part of his *sadhana,* or spiritual disciplines.

As we have noted, OM is pronounced thus: A-U-M-M-M-M. And then, repeated as an incantation, it becomes gradually: O-M-M-M-M ... O-M-M-M-M. It is the most common, the most universal sound. It is the sound of the sea, of waves breaking. We hear it in the thunder, in the wind, in the lion's roar. It is the sound of silence, and of waterfalls. It is the sound of traffic, airplanes, engines, dynamos, of bees humming. A dog baying at the moon makes that sound.

According to Vivekananda, OM is the irreducible sound-pattern that the throat can make. It stands for the totality of sounds, names, and words that can be humanly voiced. It is both idea and word—the word being necessary to evoke the idea in the mind. We want to think of God, of the highest conception we have, and hence we need a sound that stands for all sounds: OM. No other sound can be more basic. OM contains within itself the manifest and the unmanifest. The *Mandukya Upanishad* describes how the three sounds *A-U-M* represent the three levels of consciousness: waking, dreaming, and dreamless sleep. Beyond these there is the Fourth:

> Beyond the senses, beyond the understanding, beyond all expression is the Fourth. It is pure unitary consciousness....
>
> The Fourth, the Self, is OM, the indivisible syllable. In it the manifold universe disappears.... Whosoever knows OM, the Self, becomes the Self.[12]

Before and after the sound is the silence of the unmanifested reality. The Fourth level is silence, the silence of the space *between* sounds. OM points to that silence, but it is also the sound of life, of manifestation, of will in action, of the logos. In the *Maitri Upanishad*, we read:

> There are two ways of contemplation of Brahman: in sound and in silence. By sound we go to silence. The sound of Brahman is OM. With OM we go to the End: the silence of Brahman. The End is immortality, union, and peace.[13]

We have two symbols—silence and OM—each pointing to the other. Silence is symbolic of the Godhead.

OM is believed to be the sound of the creative power, of the Divine Will in action. OM is the sound of the Deity—at least, that which we can pronounce. Yogis are said to hear it in their meditation. Not only in Hindu and Buddhist traditions, but also in Christian traditions: Eastern Orthodoxy has had the sound HOM for centuries.

"Whosoever knows OM, the Self, becomes the Self,"[14] says the seer of the *Mandukya Upanishad*. OM can be viewed as a handle by which we seize hold of the thought of the Deity; without a handle it is difficult to open the door. OM is a mantram, a sacred or inspired sound that is repeated to evoke to the mind a sense of that reality we are seeking to know directly. It stands for the Beyond, the Reality within, the Divine. There are many other mantrams as well. We may prefer to repeat the name of Buddha, or of Jesus, or Krishna, or of some other name that represents the Divine. Whatever is congenial to us we should use. But in lieu of some special partiality, many find OM acceptable because it symbolizes the Godhead in the most impersonal and universal way.

PERSONAL AND IMPERSONAL REALITY

What we are seeking, however, is not necessarily an impersonal reality alone: It is both personal and impersonal, depending upon how we are attracted to it. We may be drawn to a personal Being, a personal God. So have many others. There is no reason why the personal and the impersonal cannot be combined. In fact, Vedanta doesn't exclusively dwell on the impersonal, although that is its major emphasis. It recognizes that there are other approaches.

We may wonder how the Godhead can be both personal and impersonal at the same time. To draw from one of Ramakrishna's parables, the ocean in its impersonal aspect is serene and motionless; it is vast and infinite, like Brahman in its inactive, impersonal state. But the ocean also has times of great activity when waves break out of it. At these times, the ocean seems to be made up of the ocean *and* the waves. The ocean is the impersonal Godhead and the waves are personal representations of the Divine. So here we have the introduction of the personal Being, the Ocean appearing as the waves—as both. Both are real.

Thus Brahman is initially the Absolute in its inactive stage—a potentiality only. The personal God, or *Ishvara,* is that emanation from Brahman which creates the world, the power of creation. But behind the personal God is something still greater: Brahman, the Godhead. Creation is one aspect of It. If you have creation, you have destruction too; where there's life, there's death. The impersonal Godhead is eternally beyond these pairs of opposites.

So Brahman has a destructive aspect as well—the Godhead brings the universe back into Itself. In the *Mundaka Upanishad,* Brahman is compared to a spider that projects the universe out of itself in its creative mode, the way a spider projects its web. The web and the spider are of the same substance, and we are in that web, we *are* that web. But eventually the spider brings the web back into itself; as the universe, finishing a cycle, is brought back into Brahman. This is what we call the destructive mode. Hence we have Brahman, and the world of emanation—the impersonal and the personal, the world of creation as well as destruction—the grand design.

NECESSITY OF STRUGGLE

Fire, though present in the firesticks, is not perceived until one stick is rubbed against another. The Self is like that fire: it is realized in the body by meditation on the sacred syllable OM.

> Let your body be the stick that is rubbed, the sacred syllable OM the stick that is rubbed against it. Thus shall you realize God, who is hidden within the body as fire is hidden in the wood.
>
> Like oil in sesame seeds, butter in cream, water in the riverbed, fire in tinder, the Self dwells within the soul. Realize Him through truthfulness and meditation.
>
> Like butter in cream is the Self in everything. Knowledge of the Self is gained through meditation. The Self is Brahman. By Brahman is all ignorance destroyed.[15]

Vedanta is not content with a single image. The rishis double and triple their strokes, as in the above quotation. They are enraptured with this Reality and cannot desist: "Let your body be the stick that is rubbed." What else is it? It is like fire—this imprisoned splendor that we have to liberate.

Rubbing means that we have to work for our reward. It won't do to sit back and wait for it. Friction involves struggle. The two sticks struggle with each other, as we struggle with the mind, with our life, to awaken the same fire.

Fire in sticks is one image; another is oil in sesame seeds. The next time you buy sesame seeds think of the essential oil hidden in them. Then: "like butter in cream...[so] the Self dwells within the soul."

Cream is the ordinary mind, which is neither one thing nor another. It is a mixture of elements lacking its own reality. We can't function well if our mind is like cream. Cream tends to join itself to other things and loses its character. So our creamy minds—as Ramakrishna said—mix with the world's influences and we lose remembrance of what we are. But if we churn the cream through spiritual practice, meditative disciplines, then gradually we get butter—the Self. What was cream is now butter. This butter—our purified mind, identical with the Self—is sent into the waters of the world. But now it floats; that is, it retains its integrity. Whereas, cream is mixed and is lost; butter remains itself.

6

Mind and Meditation

Knowledge of the Self is gained through meditation. The Self is Brahman....

To realize God, first control the outgoing senses and harness the mind.[16]

"To realize God, first control the outgoing senses...." The first thing we are to do in meditation is control the senses that are still attuned to worldly experience—to the body, to our job, to people, to relationships—but the means to do this are not specified.

There are two ways to struggle with the senses as this aphorism asks us to do. One way is through willpower. As we sit for meditation, we feel these distractions, memories, and attachments of all kinds; we grit our teeth and exercise our willpower to force the mind away from them, but this is not the recommended way because it gives more power to the problem.

The preferred method is to preoccupy the mind with a chosen concept or thought that will do the work of controlling the senses for us. The senses are aware of all the distractions, so we have to practice gently and steadily controlling them, not so much by forcing them to be attentive but giving them something to attend to themselves—in other words, not by willpower but by substituting one thought for another. We fill our minds with the thought of Truth instead of the thoughts that habitually fill it now.

The devotional person can meditate on the idea that God is real, God is here. Even though we might not feel it, we imagine that this is the case; it's a kind of autosuggestion. But isn't that faking it? No, the mind already has been exposed to auto-suggestions of all kinds, such as God is far away, He is in heaven. That is pure autosuggestion, isn't it? That is what is false. So we use another kind of hypnosis to drive away the hypnosis that was forced on us—that of God being distant. Now we have another hypnosis, which is that God is real, God is close by. Wouldn't we prefer this one, based on the experience of mystics and saints who say that the Lord is with us? Then, as we cultivate the thought that God is close to us, at some point we feel a sense of presence and begin to realize that this is true. All we need is the first glimmer of presence to remind us that it isn't hypnosis, but a reality based on sound authority.

So when we are meditating and the senses are pulling us out toward distractions—memories, desires, cravings, things we have to do later in the day, and all that—we bring these things to the bar of the one thought that the Lord is here, the Spirit is with me.

There's the body, the mind, and the Spirit—three realities. We are aware of the first two, but rarely aware of the third. We believe in the Spirit and hope to realize it some day, but we don't know it yet. We only know the body and the mind. The saints and sages have said there is a Spirit. Who are we to say they weren't speaking the truth? If we pray there's a Spirit, cultivate it, affirm it, and invoke it, then when these distractions come, they come in the midst of this thought that fills the room and fills our minds: the Spirit is present, the Lord is all. That is the thought of Truth. By giving Truth to the mind rather than its habitual thoughts, we can control the senses in meditation.

Another thought of Truth that is even better is that all is one. There's only the Self, only the Lord. There is only the Spirit. Everything that exists is One. Could it be that the Self in me is the same Self in others? Are we all just one Being and one Self? Is it true that our bodies, our names, and other forms deceive us, making us all feel we're not one, but many? Is this just an illusion? Underneath this is a beautiful idea that seems true. If it only were true. So we think on these ideas and fill our minds with this provisional thought that there is only one Truth, one Spirit, one Self, one Being. When the distractions come, temptations are robbed of their appeal. They are robbed of their power because we bring them into the neutralizing presence of this true thought and therefore we don't have to use willpower against them. Substitution and not resistance or suppression is recommended. Don't suppress, but substitute. Suppression wears us out.

> Then meditate upon the light in the heart of the fire—
> meditate, that is, upon pure consciousness as distinct
> from the ordinary consciousness of the intellect. Thus the
> Self, the Inner Reality, may be seen behind physical
> appearance.[17]

What we think of as consciousness is usually our awareness of objects, books, people, ideas ... *other* things. A phase of meditation is the emptying or detaching of the mind from this automatic association of itself with surface phenomena; in this way we find out what the mind truly is. We have to detach it from the interchangeable and expendable objects that seem to make up our reality, which the mind, standing behind them, greedily fastens on.

In other words, we have to train the mind, and instruct it. If left to itself, the mind runs after everything. It has to be trained, like the body. The body can't be left to its own designs; otherwise we grow lazy, overweight, tamasic, sick. We have to discipline the body and the mind, too. Who is the instructor? Something *behind* the mind. It's not the Supreme Self, but its deputy, the Atman or soul—that aspect of the Supreme within that we can get hold of. It is an extension of that Light into our empirical world. Little by little, as we purify the mind through spiritual disciplines, we feel it growing and getting stronger, and we may come to feel that it is the Divine Self actually guiding us. Then we lose sight of it and return to guiding ourselves. But as we persist in spiritual practice, it becomes clear again, and we feel the presence once more. It is a long process. Eventually, the saint doesn't feel he or she is doing anything as an ego-self, as a separate self. The saint is a kind of machine, and the Divine Itself is the operator.

And so we grow to higher and higher levels. Even in worldly terms we pass into advancing stages during which our criteria of joy change with every step. Thus it is possible to forsake our ego control for the sake of divine control—and get accustomed to that kind of joy too.

Meditate, then, upon Pure Consciousness Itself as distinct from what the intellect thinks is ordinary consciousness. Pure Consciousness—*that* is the true "I." That is the "I" that Christ referred to when he said: "I am the Way, the Truth, and the Life." Buddha also: "I have experienced the Infinite, I am Awakened." Others have had a similar experience of a consciousness that knows itself to be the Supreme Consciousness individualized, but not different from It. When this is known the experiencer feels he or she is one with God. If such a person is of a certain temperament, he or she is apt to stand up in front of a crowd and say this—and thereby end up in prison or on a cross, which has happened more than once in history.

> Hear all ye children of immortal bliss, also ye gods who dwell in the high heavens: Follow only in the footsteps of the illumined ones. And by continuous meditation merge both mind and intellect in the eternal Brahman. The glorious Lord will be revealed to you.[18]

Swetasvatara calls to us: "Hear all ye children of immortal bliss." That is the beautiful name in the Upanishads given to us: *children of immortal bliss.* Not only human beings but "also ye gods who dwell in the high heavens"—the gods are also asked to listen to the call to "follow only in the steps of the illumined ones." If the gods want to know what the truth is, they have to come to earth and follow in the footsteps of the saints and sages.

When an individual merges "both mind and intellect in the eternal Brahman" such a person is the fount of all desire. He or she is the fulfiller, not merely the recipient. The knower of Brahman *is* That—what he or she has been seeking.

We may not care for this lofty doctrine. It may not be our preferred food. But there is something haunting about it. It insists in the most unequivocal way that we have the capacity to know Truth directly. We are not used to such an uncompromising approach. We are oriented in a different way. But even as an intellectual framework there is something to be said for it as we pursue our meditations and practices. For many it may be an alternative to what Zen, for example, has to offer.

Zen

Zen is for those of us who are interested strictly in practices unfettered by belief, metaphysics, or philosophy. Zen appeals to the person who doesn't want any of these things— God, faith, and so on—but instead wants something different.

For thousands of years people have put their faith in philosophy and abstractions. Zen speaks to the need to find a different way—and it is sanctioned by Buddha himself. Zen is an option available to those who must travel along another path, following a practice that emphasizes technique and puts a minimal faith in the Zen teacher who says, "Do this and see where it takes you—believe nothing until you experience it yourself." There is something exhilarating in that approach.

But for those of us who can still stand the burden of belief and philosophy, Vedanta is the chief alternative—although there are others. On the abundant smorgasbord of

That Thou Art

modern religious options everything is available. Whatever you want, it is there. It is the truth in you that will bring you to the goal. That is why the authentic religions are really inspired; it is not the truth in *them* but the truth in us. *Tat Tvam Asi. That Thou Art.* The truth is in *us,* and we recognize it when we read the scriptures. We respond to that. You and I are the proof of the scriptures. The scriptures are full of wisdom; the wisdom is there, but it is lifeless without us. If Christ is not within you, how can you respond to him? It is the Christ within us that makes us respond to his life. It is the same with all the prophets, and all religious truths.

Truth has to be felt first. We may not have had direct experience of it necessarily, but we have to intuit it. The truth-organ is always there, always active, even though we haven't known Brahman, or the Godhead. This should guide us when someone is advocating a path to follow. If someone wants to teach us religion or spirituality, we should think and pray and meditate about it. We need to nourish this ever-alert organ of truth within so that we can use it with confidence to determine whether we are being guided properly or not, particularly with today's New Age movement that has such a variety of teachers.

The scriptures affirm that there *is* an organ of truth. Buddha himself, although he talks little about things to believe, says that the Buddha-nature is in you. That is very
Each Religion A Path much the same as what the Upanishads stress—only the terms vary. People came to Buddha and said (as they did to Christ), "You are different; you are the greatest." "I have trodden a certain path," he answered, "I have had a certain experience—of the Buddha-nature. I have reached the infinite, you can too. I am no longer Gautama, I am Buddha—the spiritually enlightened. You, too, have the same potential in you."

Isn't that similar to what the Upanishads are urging? You too have that in you—bring it out. Buddha simply used another way to express it.

So we are the proof of that reality, which is why each major religion will bring us to the goal. All we have to do is believe in our religion and practice it faithfully — with understanding — and it will bring us to perfection, if that is what we want. For it is the inner perfection it will stir up and the truth within that will be realized. A particular religion is simply the set of tools provided us, the doctrines that may help, and the philosophical framework that may enable us to kindle the Divine fire within.

The fire is not in any religion, but in you. A particular religion provides a way of rubbing the sticks together so that with a minimum of faith something will happen.

But we can't be jumping from one path to another. There is a time for that initially — a time to compare, to investigate. After a few months or a few years we should stop and, according to Ramakrishna, dig one well. Otherwise we will never dig a *deep* well. We start to dig in one place, then after a while someone says, "You still haven't reached water yet? You're digging in the wrong place; come over here." We follow his advice and get no-where. The best way is to dig deeper, where you began — providing your effort has some kind of sanction behind it. You need to dig where people who have come before you have reached the truth; some saint or prophet has dug in that place. In other words, you cannot just create your own religion. Our mind has to be *convinced* that our chosen path has produced perfect souls. If the conviction hasn't penetrated to the depths of the mind, we will reach that point in our meditation when the unprotected mind will keep us from advancing further.

So whatever faith you hold, embrace it fully, making sure that you believe it has produced great saints and leads you to the truth when earnestly followed. All the important religions have this to their credit, Zen among them. It has produced saints, unquestionably, as has Vedanta, Christianity, Sufism, and Judaism.

THE VITAL FORCE

> Control the vital force. Set fire to the Self within by the practice of meditation.[19]

Here an element of yoga or practice is brought into the text; we are asked to "control the vital force." The vital force, or in Sanskrit terms, *prana,* is not just the sexual energy, although that is part of it. Prana is the cosmic energy that pulses every moment in this world of becoming, of change and development. This energy flows through everything, especially through the mind, the body, and the will, where it takes different forms, and names. For example, it's called *kundalini* when we think of it in terms of the spiritual energy coiled at the base of the spine. It's called *sexual drive* when we think of it as sexual energy. It's called *breath* when we think of it as the power that gives us life. It's the digestive energy when metabolizing food. Prana has different names as it takes different functions.

The domain of Brahman is beyond energy, as is the soul. However, energy is necessary for the realization of pure Being. Prana is this energy in the universe, telescoped and concentrated in us as the will, which we feel at all levels. It is willpower—the energy of the will—mental energy, physical energy, and sexual energy. It is all one energy that we can use in different ways.

The gunas are also forms of this energy. Tamas is the energy of darkness, of indolence, in which a person's will is completely concentrated on depression, on delusion. Rajas is the imaginative,

ego-fed energy that says, "I want to build houses; I want to recon-
struct a city; I want to *change things*." This guna has both desirable
and less desirable aspects. Finally, sattva is the energy of the
higher mind, or the will that controls the two lesser forces and
holds them poised.

So prana is the one energy that flows through the whole
cosmos. In the individual this energy of will is called the ego
when it becomes the driving force of self-assertiveness. Normally
this energy is scattered in all different directions, but the saint
gets hold of this same immense energy, collects it, and turns it
inward toward the Self. To reach this Self you need a tremendous
driving force for the will. The ordinary will is like a baby trying
to scale Mount Everest. To go to the mountain of the Self we
need a lot of strength and energy. As it is, we waste our energy
and dissipate it in so many ways. For example, the sexual drive
and the ego drive between them command and consume almost
all of our energy supply. But the saint gets hold of this massive
energy like an apple in his or her hand and through willpower
drives it and coordinates it inward. We don't have the ability to
do that, although, we may try. The intention, the wish is there,
but the wish has insufficient will, strength, and energy. By living
the spiritual life for some years the energy will be gradually
collected so that we have more than a wish then, we have strength
and will. It's all there; it's always one. We just have to transform
it from its present form, following nature and creatureliness, to
make it follow our spiritual will and the way to enlightenment.

This transformation takes place through the energy that is
the means whereby the instruments of the soul express themselves. Energy is the means the soul has for exerting itself in

critical moments, as though to say: "I don't want any more of those other things. I want to be free. I want to know myself, I want a different existence." This shift in our thinking is evidence of the higher will (the deputy of the soul) exerting itself at these crucial times as it shakes everything up. For instance, when someone close to us dies and we are plunged in grief, and ask ourselves, "What is this life anyway? Here I am, full of ambition, restless to succeed—but what does it all mean?" A burning fire of renunciation grips us. Alas, it doesn't endure, but it is an intimation from the depths. We haven't willed it consciously; we are not used to it; and we haven't identified with it. It is a grace given to us—a new perspective.

Precious moments such as these come to us in emergencies and during spiritual hours—alas, they are all too fleeting. We have to use spiritual practices to make them last so that we progress to the point where we can finally see that we don't have to be at the mercy of the gunas and the *outgoing current,* the way we have been.

If we don't use this energy, it will use us. Which is it going to be? It's been using us up through drives and attachments.

So how are we to control such a vast energy? It is during meditation that we start to control it. But as we sit for meditation, a restlessness comes over us—the force is not used to being checked. Eventually, however, it becomes our friend. We have no real enemies in the spiritual life; it is only that we are not familiar with these forces. Anything that is sufficiently unfamiliar to us seems like an enemy. But to know all is to forgive all. If we know enough about anything, we lose our sense of estrangement.

The vital force seems to be our enemy because it wants to prevent meditation. We become anxious; we try to bring it to heel. We try to concentrate our powers on a center, but our mind—indeed, our entire system—is not used to such activity. Whole books could be written on this problem. The Upanishads simply say that we must control the vital force; there is little elaboration on how we can do this.

Why is that? As noted earlier, the Upanishads were meant to be expounded by a living guru. The teacher would say, for example, "Control the vital force," and then spend many hours elucidating this idea. In the *Swetasvatara Upanishad* these truths are simply set down in a notation, and we have to find out how to do the rest—control prana as it surges through the body, through the mind, through the senses. Sometimes the restlessness is in the mind, and this is the chief obstacle. The body's restlessness is rather quietly tamed. The mind is the problem: It seizes on the energy of the vital force and becomes obsessed with it. It takes months—or years—before we can calm the mind and have any real success in meditation.

> Unite the light within you with the light of Brahman. Thus will the source of ignorance be destroyed, and you will rise above karma.[20]

The light of Brahman is the light that we are seeking, and the light that we develop, the light within, is like a surrogate, a deputy, a stand-in that draws its luminous quality from the true luminescence further within.

Going Beyond Karma

What we have to show for developing this inner light is a kind of moral and spiritual growth we sense as our character gets more enlightened. When we've developed it sufficiently we can, in meditation, unite that light with the other light of Brahman, which is known as the mystical experience.

"Thus will the source of ignorance be destroyed." What is the source of ignorance? A feeling of separation between you and the Deity where you feel this separation is real—that is the seed of ignorance or the seed of what the Upanishadic scriptures call evil. You have to destroy that seed and then "you will rise above karma." Notice the subtlety in that sentence. Karma here for the first time is equated with ignorance. Karma is in the sphere of the mind, which is the realm of ignorance, of change, causation—sowing and reaping—the realm of the senses, of the phenomenal world. We believe in all this, and have to suffer. But isn't it real? Yes, it's real—but in the end it's not real because we go beyond it. Where is our karma then? It's like the weather we had last winter; the karma that we've worked our way through is no longer operative.

According to the Upanishads, karma is produced by our misconception of our separateness from God. The moment we know that we are one with the Lord, we no longer produce karma.

Meditate on Brahman with the help of the syllable OM. Cross the fearful currents of the ocean of worldliness by means of the raft of Brahman—the sacred syllable OM.

With earnest effort hold the senses in check. Controlling the breath, regulate the vital activities. As a charioteer holds back his restive horses, so does a persevering aspirant hold back his mind.[21]

Meditate on your ideal of reality. Strive "with earnest effort." Fire can be drawn out from the wood only with earnest effort, the cream churned only by the discipline of friction.

"With earnest effort hold the senses in check. Controlling the breath, regulate the vital activities." Controlling the breath is

**Meditation and
Breath Control**

a convenient way to get hold of the vital force and the vital activities. Prana functions most intimately through the breath. In fact, the best way to get control of the energy that is disturbing us is via the breath—both in meditation and at any other time. The respiratory power is the subtlest and most concentrated way this energy functions in the whole system. If you can breathe slowly and rhythmically in meditation, you can control prana.

During meditation, ordinary breathing—in and out through the nostrils with the mouth closed—is the best way. While seated breathe slowly and rhythmically about six or ten times before the meditation begins. This will quiet the mind. It won't work completely, but it is a step in the right direction. Regulate your breath in this manner, and not by some special method of breath control you may have read about. Other methods can be practiced with a qualified teacher; otherwise there is a danger of disturbing the mind.

Not only in meditation, but also whenever you are troubled or agitated, if you can get control of your breath, you can bring yourself to a collected state. Simply sit down, stop the body's movement, and breathe regularly through the nostrils for a few minutes, preferably while repeating OM.

Breath is not the vital force, but a manifestation of this hidden and invisible energy called prana; if we can gain control over such a key area we can control the vital force.

DIFFERENT PATHS TO REALIZATION

The yogi experiences directly the truth of Brahman by realizing the light of the Self within. He is freed from all impurities—he the pure, the birthless, the bright.[22]

The path of yoga is the path of practice. A *yogi* or *yogini* is one who practices yoga. When one knows Brahman, he or she is freed from impurities and becomes "the birthless," becomes *That*.

The Indian sages urge you to keep this great thought in the back of your mind as you meditate—that you are one with that on which you meditate. The part of you that thinks you are separate is the element in your nature you are trying to purify and transform through spiritual practices. *That Art Thou.* India's philosophy identifies itself with that single sentence.

Yet, as noted, there is a personal God in Vedanta also. On one hand there is absolute Vedanta, the monistic, nondual, advaita approach to the Godhead that claims that Brahman and you yourself—your soul—are one. There is also qualified nondualism, which asserts that absolute nondualism may be true, but that individual souls exist, divine in their essence, who are not exactly *identical* with Brahman, but rather are part of Brahman.

On the other hand, there is the personal approach of dualistic Vedanta, which can be pursued against the impersonal background. For instance, we may worship a **The Personal God in Vedanta** personal God, a saint, or a divine incarnation, because of our own temperament, and at the same time we place this devotional impulse against the wider perspective of the impersonal Reality. That Being whom we worship—or that Christ, that Buddha—is a channel to something beyond. And what is that which is beyond the personal God? And where is it? Devotional figures strengthen us along the way, but they are not the end, not the destination: neither Christ nor Buddha would say that he was.

Vedanta is preoccupied with what lies beyond *them*. It admits divine incarnations, or avatars, and says that this is part of the grace of Brahman itself. If we didn't have these avatars from time to time, we would never come to realize what the Truth is. We could live for billions of lifetimes and it would never occur to us—because even after we've heard it, it sounds strange and abstract. If it weren't for the appearance of great souls who come periodically and announce the Truth with such unique and powerful impact, we would be lost, like comets falling through the darkness of space. It is through their influence that, in the hope of experiencing the same that they have known, we are led to turn within.

Thus Vedanta is not exclusively impersonal. Its philosophical substructure is based on nondualism, but it recognizes that human beings have their temperamental leanings, their tastes and differences, and the personal God appeals to many of them. The ideal combination for some would be to meditate on the personal aspects of the Deity against this impersonal background, focused in the region of the heart. If the inner light of devotion is awakened, there is simultaneously a sense of uniting with the All—hence the ecstasy, the unutterable nature of the samadhi experience that sages and mystics tell us about.

7

 Maya and the Nature of Reality

The one absolute, impersonal Existence, together with his inscrutable Maya, appears as the divine Lord, the personal God.[23]

Maya is a difficult concept. Even Hindus don't agree on what they mean by the term. In any case, Maya is a power in the world that veils the Truth from our eyes. Why this should be, we don't know yet. It is inscrutable—until we have the mystical experience, and then more light is shed upon the path.

Maya at first seems to be a devilish, perverse power—part of William Blake's world of contraries. It is what some religions have called Satan. In part it is that, but it is also a power of confusion and delusion; it's the element that upsets things. It is—as Ralph Waldo Emerson called it in a witty phrase—the "unscheduled ingredient." In common parlance Maya is evoked in the saying that if anything can possibly go wrong, it will. We plan carefully but invariably there's something we overlook that upsets things. Why is that? We never think of everything. This is part of Maya.

Another word for Maya is *Prakriti,* a term used in the Sankhya philosophy, one of the other main systems of Hindu philosophy. Prakriti, which is nature or matter, cohabits the universe with *Purusha,* which represents the Spirit or Soul. In this school of thought, Prakriti and Purusha are the two ultimate realities. When they interact with each other, the result is creation. *Prakriti* in Sanskrit means "that which is to be controlled," and *Purusha* means "shining light." So nature, in particular our inner nature, or the mind, is to be controlled so that the light of the Spirit can shine through.

In the *Swetasvatara Upanishad*, Maya is described as the power that unites mind and matter. It seems to be something that Brahman *puts out* as a test of our ability to negotiate the sea of Maya, in order for us to get beyond Maya. It is the *opposition* provided in our struggle to reach the Truth. Even so, it is a divine power, a veiling component of Brahman.

SPIRITUAL AWAKENING

Said the great seer Swetasvatara:

I have known, beyond all darkness, that great Person of golden effulgence. Only by knowing him does one conquer death. There is no other way of escaping the wheel of birth, death, and rebirth.

"Person" here refers not to an individual but evokes the sense of some essential personality that undergirds everyone. In addition to the varieties of temperaments, karmas, and talents we have, there's one Personality, so to speak, or one Personhood, or Selfhood behind all of us. And to know that is to know the Self. "Only by knowing him does one conquer death. There is no other way of escaping the wheel of birth, death, and rebirth." It continues:

There is nothing superior to him, nothing different from him, nothing subtler or greater than he. Alone he stands, changeless, self-luminous; he, the Great One, fills this universe.[24]

"There is nothing superior to him, nothing different from him." Nothing is different from Him—that is why when we give money to a beggar we must give it carefully, in the right spirit, otherwise the beggar won't accept it, but will resent us, hate us, and feel superior to us. We have to do it in the right way. Why? Because the Self is in him, too, but we forget that. That is why beggars *can* be choosers, actually, because they are the same as us; they are simply performing a different role.

The phrase, "Great One" here is not in the sense of a Great Being but the Great Oneness.

Then follows Swetasvatara's version of the spiritual awakening:

Full of grace, he ultimately gives liberation to all creatures.

None can be lost in *this* universe. No matter how long we should try, we can't get away from the Godhead. The Divine will follow us as far as we flee. "Full of grace, he ultimately gives liberation to all creatures." How? "By turning their faces toward himself."[25]

The Divine quickening in us is a profound mystery. In St. John's epistles we read: "We love Him, because He first loved us."[26] This might be a rendering of the *Swetasvatara* passage. That is, a spiritual awakening—some stirring in us for the Divine—is this turning of our faces toward the Truth.

Normally it would never occur to us to do it. In our nature-given personalities we are not inclined to such reversals; we have other interests and preoccupations that take up our time. At a certain point in our lives, however, we feel that something is *turning* us in a new direction. This occurs not altogether in accordance with our will, and yet not against it either. We then have to begin to struggle and *realize* Truth that has merely dawned. Nevertheless the work is started, although we cannot initiate it on our own: He turns all faces toward Himself.

> He is the Innermost Self…. He it is that reveals the purity within the heart by means of which he, who is pure being, may be reached.[27]

By the grace of God we are enabled to feel that deep within our own human habitation in the heart, in the center of our being, there's a great purity, a great goodness. If we can develop and nourish ourselves as we are in our best hours, in our best potential, it will be the means whereby pure being itself is to be reached. As we are in our True Self, we are the links to absolute purity, but not as we are in our usual unenlightened state.

> This great Being has a thousand heads, a thousand eyes, and a thousand feet. He envelops the universe. Though transcendent, he is to be meditated upon as residing in the lotus of the heart at the center of the body, ten fingers above the navel.
>
> He alone is all this—what has been and what shall be. He has become the universe.[28]

The whole world is his incarnation—which explains many things. Ethics, for one. Only Vedanta explains unselfishness: The person you are being unselfish toward is yourself, or a phase of you—not that particular body or face, but that Being. His or her being is your being. When you are selfish you wound that, the Self, not the body. In doing so you are wounding yourself because you *are* That.

This concept explains Buddhism also. Why have so much compassion toward everything—not only human beings but animals and all creatures? Buddha was willing to give up his life for a goat. When he saw a man killing a goat as a sacrifice, he protested, You should stop that—why are you doing it?

"I want to gain merit," the man said. Buddha answered, "Take *my* body—you will gain real merit."

And he offered his body to the man as a sign that he—and everyone—should stop the killing of animals as a way to gain merit. This is reverence for life. Why, exactly? It feels good and sounds good, but what is the rationale behind it? Vedanta provides us with the answer.

This concept also explains one of the main principles in William Blake's poetry: "Everything that lives is holy." Everything partakes of the Divine. Some may be in a less-developed guise, but the holiness is in their essence, not necessarily so much in their form, which is expendable. Since we are all going through a multitude of different forms, no particular form is sacred in the same way as the soul. And yet, according to Walt Whitman, the body is sacred too, reflecting the soul's divinity: The body is the garment and vehicle of the soul. So we must give it respect, even reverence—although not ultimate reverence.

"This great Being ... envelops the universe." Vedanta says it is you who envelop the universe, an exciting and yet a strange teaching. Here I am—limited, mortal, trapped in a body—and I am told *I am That:* a doctrine almost too lofty for our experience. Nevertheless there's something about it we can't shake off. Once we hear it, we never forget it.

Meister Eckhart and particularly some Sufi mystics experienced this truth and, directly upon their vision, made extravagant claims, which vexed the authorities, resulting in either their execution, exile, or excommunication. Eckhart, the great Christian mystic of the Middle Ages, was declared anathema by the Catholic Church because he said, "without me God would not know that He existed," and "the eye by which I see God is the same eye by which God sees me."

Though Brahman is transcendent, the *Swetasvatara Upanishad* says that It is also immanent and omnipresent:

> He is to be meditated upon as residing in the lotus of the heart, at the center of the body, ten fingers above the navel.[29]

That instruction is for the student who asks: Where shall I meditate, what part of the body? And the guru answers: In the region of the heart. In other words, you will reap the best results in the most sensitive area of the psyche. Brahman is everywhere—in the brain, in the hands, in the blood—but in the heart is where you find It most readily.

Ramakrishna compared Brahman to a cow. Consider the whole cow, he said, as Brahman. Every part of the cow *is* the cow: feet, head, tail, and so on. But for our purposes the udder is the essential part. It is from the udder that we receive her most precious substance. In the same way, the heart is where we try to find the omnipresent God.

According to the mystics we are walking around with this divine presence in the area of the heart, which is where Patanjali also recommends that we meditate, rather than the area of the third eye. We've all seen diagrams of the third eye, like a radiant light in the middle of the forehead, which is the popular notion of where to concentrate and meditate on. It's not necessarily wrong when you meditate in the area of the third eye, but super figures of spirituality including Patanjali, Ramakrishna, and Ramana Maharshi recommend the heart area. We should follow where the masters guide us, and not where someone has drawn a diagram and said this is the best place. Who can surpass these great teachers of mysticism that recommend the area of the heart?

"He alone," says the text, "is *all this*." Everything that can be seen or contemplated. "His hands and feet ... eyes, heads, mouths, ears are everywhere."[30]

Now the transcriber turns to poetry. It wasn't the sage Swetasvatara who wrote down these passages but one of his disciples. Typically, a great seer will not write a scripture but will merely announce his experiences and then the disciple will write them down as precious documents. Someone who feels that Brahman is doing everything will spend little time with literary art; but, if it weren't for the disciples, the craftsmen, we wouldn't have the scriptures to start with. Both are essential: the seer, and the one who records the seer's findings.

Beginning with "O Brahman Supreme!" Swetasvatara launches into a rhapsody. The lines that follow are famous:

> Thou art the fire,
> Thou art the sun...
>
> Thou art woman, thou art man,
> Thou art the youth, thou art the maiden,
> Thou art the old man tottering with his staff;
> Thou facest everywhere.
>
> Thou art the dark butterfly,
> Thou art the green parrot with red eyes...[31]

That is why saints can commune with animals and birds—they too are part of all this, emerging in the saint's consciousness out of the background of Brahman.

The mystic who has realized the Truth and is no longer identified with his or her false self awakens this reality in others. Such a person thinks of creatures encountered only in terms of manifesting that which he or she has experienced. So the mystic loves all creatures, not by an act of will, as we do, or out of a feeling that it is virtuous to do so—instead, the response flows naturally. The mystic sees other beings as parts of one divine life. Wild animals are easily tamed—not even *tamed,* which suggests a process going on, but simply *cease to be wild* in the presence of those who have transcended the wildness within themselves.

The Upanishad continues:

> Maya is thy divine consort
> Wedded to thee.
> Thou art her master, her ruler.
> Red, white, and black is she,
> Each color a guna.[32]

"Red, white, and black is [Maya], each color a guna." These are the colors of the elements—fire, water, and earth. Nature is a **Maya and** phase of Maya, the inscrutable. The gunas are **the Gunas** Maya. I fall into a state of rajas and think it is reality. It fills my horizon. That is Maya. Someone not in that position sees it for what it is. A man in the midst of drunkenness sees the whole world in that light, but someone observing him realizes he's in the grip of a tamasic seizure—that he's not himself, that it is the alcohol speaking through him. In any passion it is not the individual speaking but the passion itself, the guna.

At first glance this outlook seems to relieve us of all responsibility. But that's not really the case: With the dawn of discrimination we discover that when we feel a passion rising, whatever it may be, we tell ourselves, "I'm not going to let this emotion possess me, because when I do I become a stranger to myself, I lose myself." A heavy responsibility remains.

Even sattva, serene and spiritual, is not the end, as we've seen. Many people, spiritual seekers of a kind, feel they have reached an advanced stage when they attain sattva—but that is only a phase too. Sattva is far from being the end of the road. Although in comparison to rajas and tamas it seems to be enlightenment, sattva is actually well within the realm of Maya.

Consider certain intellectuals with a good moral background, of definite sattvic tendencies, far from being in the grip of tamas or of rajas, they seem to be spiritual individuals. In fact, the state they have reached is the last development of a phenomenal, karma-grounded character—the ego-personality *before* it becomes truly spiritual. If we are brought up well, have a good education, and enjoy a superior intelligence, we would tend to be like that. But this is not the spiritual character—the individual is still basically egocentric.

In other words, spiritual realization is entirely different from a moral and ethical mindset. Nevertheless we must reach that point of moral and ethical development before we can go beyond and discover the essentials of mysticism.

TWO BIRDS ON THE TREE OF LIFE

Towards the end of the *Swetasvatara Upanishad* we have the brilliant image of two beautiful and inseparable birds on the tree of life:

> Like two beautiful birds,
> Golden of plumage,
> Companions inseparable,
> Perched high up on the branches
> Of the selfsame tree....[33]

One bird is perched at the top of the tree, serene, all-knowing, poised in its own magnificence—the soul. The other is the phenomenal self, the ego creation we call into being by wrong identification of the soul with passing elements: the eternal identified with the noneternal, in the words of Shankara. This second bird tastes the sweet fruits of the tree, and then the bitter fruits. It represents the empirical, bound aspect of our existence, where we turn from the sweet to the bitter, and are tossed back and forth, lifetime after lifetime, between these contraries, unable to see what the truth is. Gradually we work our way up the tree by the very power of these experiences, driven by the feelings of despair, exasperation, and restlessness created in the soul: "When am I going to quit this endless round of pain and pleasure? When am I going to do something different? When am I going to be better?" Little by little we rise ever higher.

Meanwhile at the top of the tree the other bird still sits there, regal and detached, untouched by change, waiting for us. We look up every so often and see it—still so remote, so unreachable—as we are tossed this way and that, caught in the conflict of contraries, of the bitter and the sweet of life, but gradually moving up.

Finally the second bird reaches the top and discovers it was one with the other, magnificent bird all the time; they are not two, but one. Then this whole strange process of Maya turns out to have been a delusion, merely an arena whereby the bird on the lower branches, through this process of becoming, would come to realize itself for what it is.

> Thou alone art ...
> Of all religions thou art the source.
> The light of thy knowledge shining,
> There is neither day nor night, nor being
>   nor nonbeing —
> Thou alone art.[34]

"Thou alone art." The scribe repeats this phrase because of its importance. That is what the mystics of the Upanishads discover, that the Lord is all that exists. If that is true, that will explain everything. It explains the contraries as being necessary; behind them there stands the resolving, synthesizing One. It is everything. That is another aspect of their grand thought: The Lord is all that exists, the Lord is the soul, the soul is all that exists, and you are the soul, therefore you are all that exists. So we have our morality and ethics all built into a single sentence — it's all there — how to live, why we should live this way, why we should meditate. Without meditation we can't believe these ideas. We may feel that they are too good to be true, that they are just theories. So meditation will help us to believe them and eventually enable us to act upon them.

"Thou alone art." This is the chief idea in the Upanishads, on which we find a hundred variations. And with it — the union, the identity of the soul with That.

> Neither male nor female art thou, nor neuter;
> Whatever form thou assumest,

That thou art.[35]

Male and female are terms by which the reason attempts to understand truth through logical categories. But the Supreme is

The Illusion of Opposites beyond this mode of experience. It is said to be neither existence nor nonexistence. It cannot be described, as Buddha reported. Male and female are merely contraries, not realities—an integral part of our illusion.

These terms are categories, parts of the *grand* illusion. Although on the surface they appear to be separate, underneath they are the same reality. Their function and roles are different, just as the contraries—tigers and lambs, sun and moon, light and darkness—have roles as different as can be so that the full significance of life may be experienced, or as much of it as possible. If there was but one function, the truth would not benefit by the lack of friction between them.

Male and female have the same purpose and the same destiny at stake. It is as though they chose their function to bring each to the Truth. The male cannot know the meaning of life without the seeming conflict of the female, mirroring realities beyond his present range. Her mode of apprehending the Divine is simply not his. He approaches It differently than she does (when he approaches It at all) and both need what the other has. Each lacks something; the ideal is to possess what *both* have. And that is to be achieved *after* the spiritual life has been undertaken.

Perhaps the most effective illusions we have created are those of life and death. We feel they are different. To mystics, however, there is no essential difference; the same reality is there in each. In one room it is seen as life. In another room it is seen in another guise. Death leads to life, which leads to death, which leads to life. A room leads to a room, and to still another room. It is all one Existence, now seen as life, now seen as death—if there is anything called death.

"Whatever form thou assumest, that thou art." Here the Upanishad reminds us of the sanctity of all forms. Since Brahman has become everything, each person is an embodiment of the essence within them. Just as a raging fire takes the form of each thing it consumes—house, tree, car, man—so Brahman takes the form of everything it gives life to. This explains how we can see Brahman as a man or woman—and as a tree or an animal:

> Thou dost pervade the universe,
> Thou art consciousness itself.[36]

Another image often favored is that of the bonfire, with its billions of sparks, each of which has the same substance and nature of the bonfire itself. Brahman's fire has projected worlds out of its being, and each creature in the universe is Brahman in the way the spark is the fire. The spark is not the bonfire but its *nature* is the same. The difference is that the sparks tend to vanish, while the fire remains. In this Hindu metaphor the sparks fly off into darkness and do not disappear, but they question what they are doing, who they are, and where they are going. Eventually, they make the long pilgrimage back to the source, a journey of innumerable incarnations that continues until each spark rejoins the fire and discovers it was fire all along (as the second bird in the tree discovered its identity) and not the many other things it thought it was.

A few more lines in the continuing invocation to Brahman:

> Thou, womb and tomb of the universe,
> And its abode.

Womb: It begets the universe. Tomb: Everything returns unto it.

Abode: It sustains everything during the long process between.

Thou art the eternal among noneternals.

Everything is impermanent in the world except the Self. The Self is Brahman, according to the Hindus. This is a liberating

The Self and Brahman

approach for many who think of Brahman not as an indescribable Absolute but as something we can all feel. We may not know what the Self *is* but we know what it *feels* like. That Self within you—although still not illumined—is *That*. If we never know this, we will never be free from bondage.

> Can a man roll up the sky
> Like a piece of skin?
> Can he end his misery
> And not know Thee? [37]

The *Swetasvatara Upanishad* concludes with the highest impossibility you can imagine: "Can a man roll up the sky like a piece of skin?" That would be the height of impossibility. "Can he end his misery and know not Thee?" Can a man end his misery without knowing God? No, he can't. That would be equally impossible to imagine. The sage sees this so clearly that he's appalled that others don't see it. We think we can end our misery and we try many things, but without success. The sage assumes our state of misery, but also assumes the coming states of glory: the state of bliss and realization that we have been vouchsafed. We must keep both these ideas in mind at the same time as we make our way through the forest of life. We remember our limitations, miseries, and sufferings, and others who are suffering the same way, but also where we are moving toward, where our divine potential lies and what we really are: Children of Immortal Bliss.

8

The Chandogya and
Brihadaranyaka Upanishads

Each Upanishad stresses the principal idea common to all of them, which is succinctly expressed in the phrase *Thou alone art*—but presents it in its own way. In the older *Chandogya*, for example, there is a famous passage we cannot overlook. A father, Uddalaka, sends his son Svetaketu off to school to learn the knowledge of Brahman. We send our children to school to learn worldly things; we never think of asking them if they have yet learned what the knowledge of Brahman is. In the *Chandogya Upanishad*, however, Uddalaka asks exactly that question of his son Svetaketu when he returns home:

> "Have you asked for that knowledge by which we hear the unhearable, by which we perceive the unperceivable, by which we know the unknowable?"
> "What is that knowledge, sir?"[38]

That of course is the knowledge of Brahman. If you know what that is, you know what everything is. This is the clay behind all clay figures, the gold behind all the gold objects, the essence behind life, assuming all forms, inhabiting all lives, possessing all souls.

Usually we seek knowledge by taking courses, earning degrees, undergoing a long process of formal education. We have to do this to discipline the mind, and perhaps that is the main benefit that comes out of seeking an education. But the world of knowledge is so vast, with so many fields, that we can't hope to encompass even a small portion of them through that method. There aren't enough years in a lifetime.

A better method—after we've learned to *think*—is to seek the knowledge of Brahman directly. In this way we go straight to the source where all knowledge will be open to us. Instead of working from the periphery—piecemeal, mastering facts, classifying—we plunge into the center, where everything is available to the transformed consciousness. *"What is that, by knowing which, all other things may be known?"* as the *Swetasvatara Upanishad* asks.

So Uddalaka continues to instruct his son, and at length the tremendous announcement is made that:

> "All that is, has its self in Him alone. He is the truth. Of all things He is the subtle essence. He is the Self. And that, Svetaketu, That Art Thou."
>
> "Please, sir, tell me more about the Self."
>
> "Be it so, my child."[39]

The long dialogue goes on for many pages like this, until finally the mind is steeped in its whole idiom and conception of the world. Not one or two, but many illustrations are advanced, so that the mind is surrounded, as it were, by the central idea. Every possible question that can be raised is anticipated until at last the feeling arises: Perhaps there *is* something here worth meditating on.

Brahman, or the Self, cannot be an object of experience. We can experience everything else, though. Ideas can be our object, books, people, places—but not that which is timeless and super-rational, not that which is beyond the reach of the experiencing mind itself, not that which is the *Experiencer*. *Not* the Knower: the Knower cannot be known. "By whom shall the Knower be known?[40] asks Yagnavalkya, in the *Brihadaranyaka Upanishad*.

We don't attain a mystical consciousness and then discover a self separate from the self we are now. We don't come into a new mind as though into a foreign country. In a dark room you turn on the light and the darkness is gone instantly. It no longer exists. The new self is like that when it dawns: The old self is suddenly no more. The abiding mystical consciousness *is* the Self. And when we know it, the mystics say, there is a conviction that it is our true identity. It is not really strange to us; we have always known it.

What *is* strange is the half-life that we have made so familiar. Like a duck that has made land its only home, it doesn't know any other until someone introduces it to the water. This is me, it realizes; this is my reality. Then its life on land seems like a dream.

If we could think along these lines a little more than we do, we might remove the lingering suspicion that mysticism is an exotic path meant for special people—gifted or unusual or *peculiar* in some way. This kind of attitude clouds even the minds of those of us who are seekers; it's a hangover from the past. It simply is not the truth at all. Quite the opposite: The intuition of mystical reality is the awakening of our true self. When we have this experience we suddenly feel, it was me all the time—and I was thinking I was something else. How did I do it?

In the *Brihadaranyaka Upanishad,* Yagnavalkya, a well-known sage, is about to renounce the world. He has two wives: one is interested in Spirit; the other is interested in his inheritance. He gives to each what she wants—to one his possessions, to the other his knowledge. In this Upanishad Yagnavalkya is talking to Maitreyi, the wife who is interested in Spirit.

Maitreyi wants to know the Truth and asks him, what *is* the Self? Yagnavalkya says to her:

> "It is not for the sake of the husband, my beloved, that the husband is esteemed, but for the sake of the Self.

> "It is not for the sake of the wife, my beloved, that the wife is esteemed, but for the sake of the Self....

> "It is not for the sake of itself, my beloved, that anything whatever is esteemed, but for the sake of the Self....

> "Let all ignore him who thinks that anything whatever is different from the Self."[41]

He calls her "my beloved" because she is a seeker of Truth. The husband esteems the wife because of the Divine that is in her. Whether he knows it yet or not, that is the truth. Likewise it is the Self in the husband that is esteemed by the wife. Each esteems the other because of the Truth within them.

How can this insight be useful to us? In one simple way: When you go home and greet your husband or wife, think that he or she may be an embodiment of Brahman, of the Supreme, and for a few minutes relate to your loved one as an incarnation of God. Do the same with your children. There is little to lose. It is the kind of thing we have to do. We have to make experiments.

The sage might say: "Yes, it is all true, and you will find out if you try it." Relate to people as though they were God in action.

How long can we keep it up? Alas, not very long. The fault is not theirs—it is ours. The *mind* can't sustain the change. Our ordinary minds, hypnotized into thnking these people are not God but are many other things, will come to the fore and we will lapse back to where we were. But for a few minutes we can exercise control, we can impose this new vision on the mind for that interval, and whatever truth is in it should certainly emerge. We will be carrying out Christ's dictum: "Judge not according to appearances, but judge righteous judgment."[42]

A supplementary interpretation of this Upanishadic passage would remind us that every experience, every relationship, can teach us of the Divine. Falling in love or marrying, for example, enables us to understand the knowledge of God, the divine in human affairs. The awakening of love can't be understood or sanctioned by the ordinary reason. It is a mystical experience. A person truly in love resembles the mystic, if on a lesser scale. The mystic feels as the lover does—but towards everyone. That is the only difference. That is to say, the mystic feels selfless, all-loving, all-forgiving, fearless, self-sacrificing, just as we feel toward our beloved. Ordinary ego-conceptions do not prevail when we are in love; an entirely different part of our personality is involved, the mystical part. Other relationships, in the same way, can be cultivated to distill out of them their mystical truth.

"Let all ignore him," says Yagnavalkya, "who thinks that anything whatever is different from the Self." Humanity's heroes are those who have this sense of unity with others. We sense their oneness and attunement with them. We recognize that that is the thing in them we would most desire, not their power or fortune but *that* quality. Even political heroes sometimes have it to some degree, which gives them a radiance above their fellows—not to speak of the still greater moral and spiritual leaders.

Yagnavalkya continues instructing his truth-seeking wife:

> "As a lump of salt when thrown into water melts away and the lump cannot be taken out, but wherever we taste the water it is salty, even so, O Maitreyi, the individual self, dissolved, is the Eternal.... Where there is consciousness of the Self, individuality is no more."
>
> "This that you say, my lord, confuses me."[43]

It confuses all of us at first. We want wisdom, but cannot conceive of having it without our prized individuality remaining intact.

We need to free ourselves of this phantom conceit that our mutable individuality *as such*—at any given moment—is a precious thing we mustn't lose, for there is

Individuality

something else we gain in its stead, far more valuable: *ourselves*. Individuality as we think of it is merely the cocoon in which the Self lies buried.

Individuality is really a myth. It is so changeable that we don't know just what it is at any point in our life. If we lived to be 100 and were asked when our individuality was truly in flower we wouldn't know when to choose because every decade it changes—our *ego*-conception of individuality, that is, which, the sage reminds us, is not a true conception at all. The truth is that we don't know what our individuality is. Something that fluctuates so constantly, at the mercy of so many phenomena and creature influences, cannot be a satisfactory possession.

Yagnavalkya says that the realization of the Self will destroy this phantom because with the new insight we will come into an individuality in which everything is part of us. The individuality that we know now is separatist. That is what we cling to. It is egoism responding when we protest: What will happen to my individuality in mystical experience? However righteous it sounds, that is the ego speaking, loving divisions and differences; whereas, the spiritual element in us is trying to find unity and oneness.

We want to develop and polish our individuality, but keep it intact, apart from other entities. We want to cultivate it, not lose it. In mystical experience, however, we lose the egotistic sense of individuality and gain a different consciousness entirely. It is like explaining to a boy of ten about the joys of married life. He doesn't believe there are any other joys except the ones he knows. So we think our idea of individuality is the ultimate when it is only the beginning. There is something much beyond that.

The sage continues:

"As long as there is duality, one sees *the other,* hears *the other* ... one knows *the other*.... By whom shall the Knower be known?"[44]

According to the *Taittiriya Upanishad,* where there is the least idea of separation from Him, there is fear. When we know another as different from ourselves, there is fear. This fear can be removed only by the consciousness of oneness, an Upanishadic theme.

Buddhism confirms the experience of the Hindu sages with its celebration of the state of Nirvana, the Buddhist term for mystical consciousness. *Nirvana* means an extinguishing or blowing out—not of life but of *ego*-life. Does the individual cease to exist in Nirvana? Such a person continues to exist. What is destroyed is the ego. The body goes on existing. In the new consciousness everything else that we see remains: The body remains, but the inner person is transformed, the ego-individuality replaced with an infinite Presence.

We have to keep training our minds not to think that this experience has anything to do with annihilation, as we all tend to believe at first. It is simply the dissolution or extinction of the ego-power. Therefore, will mystical consciousness cause us to become nothings and lose our individuality? Quite the contrary: It will expand us to include the universe.

The individuality we hug close is trapped in a kind of shell, like the caterpillar in a cocoon. Just as the caterpillar goes through metamorphosis to break free from its cocoon to achieve the next stage of development and become a butterfly, so we have to break the encasement of the ego-consciousness. After we do this, the Infinite will not be alien to us, although it is now. The feeling of exaltation and bliss that accompanies the experience, universally attested to, is the sign of coming into our true realm.

We're attracted to the Infinite, but we're afraid of it, too. When we don't have any direct experience of something, we are a little estranged from it even as it lures us on. This is what undergirds our fear that we are going to lose our individuality. But all the sages declare that the Infinite is our actual self. The discovery will be like suddenly coming home to ourselves in a flashpoint of awareness, consuming but a single moment. It will be like illuminating a dark room — after the light appears we don't wonder where the darkness has gone, it seems never to have been. The moment the light is on, we don't conceive of darkness any longer.

This is how it is with the experience of the true self. The old self, so afraid to develop beyond its known limits, is magically wiped out, and we don't think of it any longer—just as we don't recall the darkness, which has not so much been changed as somehow fallen into nonbeing. Our true nature is Light.

9

The Katha Upanishad

The *Katha Upanishad* is one of the most popular Upanishads, and like the *Swetasvatara,* covers the principal concepts of the Vedanta philosophy in its own inimitable way. It consists of a dialogue between an exceptional youth, Nachiketa, and Yama, the King of Death. With such a sincere and worthy student as Nachiketa, "a Brahmin, like to a flame of fire," the King of Death gives spiritual knowledge and the secret of death, starting with the folowing:

> The good is one thing; the pleasant is another. These two, differing in their ends both prompt to action. Blessed are they that choose the good; they that choose the pleasant miss the goal.[45]

By *good* is meant spiritual, whereas, *pleasant* refers to the body and senses. Accordingly, the good leads to permanence and the pleasant to impermanence. When you have a choice always choose the good because if you choose the pleasant over the good with knowledge of what you are doing, it can't end well.

The Good and the Pleasant

How do we know how to choose between the good and the pleasant? "These two, differing in their ends, both prompt to action." We know by where they lead, by the consequences of the action. This will guide us if we are ever in doubt. "Blessed are they that choose the good; they that choose the pleasant miss the goal." Nachiketa has been offered all manner of pleasant objects and powers by the King of Death but has rejected them in favor of the good, the knowledge of Truth. Yama praises Nachiketa:

> The awakening which thou hast known does not come through the intellect, but rather, in fullest measure, from the lips of the wise. Blessed art thou, because thou seekest the Eternal. Would that I had more pupils like thee![46]

"The awakening which thou hast known does not come through the intellect, but ... from the lips of the wise." This idea, not unique to the *Katha Upanishad,* is that ultimately the illumined soul, the sage, can convey to the congenial, auspicious student the truth of Brahman in a special way not known through the intellect or in any other way. "Blessed art thou, because thou seekest the Eternal. Would that I had more pupils like thee!" Others seek powers and many other things; Nachiketa is one of the very few who for some mysterious reason seek the Eternal.

> The ancient, effulgent being, the indwelling Spirit, subtle, deep-hidden in the lotus of the heart, is hard to know. But the wise man, following the path of meditation, knows him, and is freed alike from pleasure and from pain.[47]

"The ancient, effulgent being" —*ancient* here means immortal, out of time. "The indwelling Spirit, deep-hidden in the lotus of the heart" —the heart represents the center of our being. The lotus of the heart refers to the heart chakra, one of the seven psychic centers or etheric yogic centers in our spiritual constitution where wheels of consciousness or spiritual energy manifest to yogis. These centers of psychic energy are apparently shaped like a lotus flower with many petals, which the yogi sees whirling. These seven zones are located along the spine, starting at the base and leading to the top of the brain; each zone is a new level of consciousness in the ascending scale of our spiritual life. As we progress spiritually, the kundalini, the cosmic energy coiled at the base of the spine, starts to move up the spine through these centers. The heart area is one of these zones. When a person's consciousness centers on the lower three chakras, he or she is concerned mainly with the body (eating, sleeping, and sense enjoyments) but when the kundalini rises to the fourth zone or the heart chakra then we know that spiritual life has begun in earnest. The statement that this is hard to know is, of course, an understatement—only yogis know what these are.

"But the wise man, following the path of meditation, knows him, and is freed alike from pleasure and from pain." Notice that it doesn't say that the wise man is freed from joy, or delight, but freed from pleasure. Pleasure is of the body; pain is of the body. But supposing the body suffers, or has cravings, the wise man rises above them easily. The body may still be prone to these, but he rises above them, and if he so wishes, is not aware of them.

> The man who has learned that the Self is separate from the body, the senses, and the mind, and has fully known him ... such a man verily attains to him, and is exceeding glad, because he has found the source and dwelling place of all felicity.[48]

"The man who has learned that the Self is separate from the body, the senses, and the mind, and has fully known him": He doesn't know Brahman fully in himself but knows him fully in terms of our human capability to know him. As long as we are embodied, we can't know him fully in his own nature since He is an infinite being: "Such a man verily attains to him, and is exceeding glad, because he has found the source and dwelling place of all felicity."

It's not surprising to find the concept of OM included in the *Katha Upanishad.*

> Of that goal which all the Vedas declare.... It is—OM. This syllable is Brahman. This syllable is indeed supreme....
>
> He who knows it obtains his desire. It is the strongest support. It is the highest symbol.[49]

OM is Brahman in the sense that before any manifestation of the creation, before any life, Brahman existed immutable, motion-**OM - The Strongest** less and increate, full of its own being. And **Support** then It decided for some reason to manifest, to body itself forth. How did this creation start? We don't know for sure; the yogis suggest that it started out with thought, then sound and then with form, in that sequence. So sound is the first manifestation of the will of the divine Brahman, which says, "I am alone, I will be many," like the playwright who wants to express himself through many characters and many stories. OM stands for the sound by which the creation is launched. "This syllable is Brahman." It is Brahman in a manner of speaking since it is the root, primal sound from which all sounds are said symbolically to derive, and that is what makes it supreme.

"He who knows it obtains his desire" —but knowing it in its innermost meaning. We have to become one with it, and unite the mind with the depths of this mantram, then we can say we know it and with this unitive knowledge we will have all our desires fulfilled. Having reached this stage, of course the desires won't be worldly desires.

"It is the strongest support." This means that if we can remember this sound in times of temptation or danger, it will cause us to escape from the danger, which will then dissolve. Why is that? This is said to be a sacred sound, and according to yogis, to have emanated from some nonhuman source, so it represents the Divine in a kind of pure and absolute way. Other names and words also represent the Divine. For example, if you believe in Christ and Buddha, their very names will rescue you. "Hallowed be thy name," said Jesus in the Lord's Prayer. He didn't say what the name was, but it probably was some mysterious mantram like OM. Jesus would have known that ultimate sound.

OM stands for that ultimate sound, and it also stands for the Supreme Reality, the power that has created everything. "It is the strongest support." So in times of danger, if we can remember and repeat this sacred sound, everything around us will be neutralized, even though we still may be shaking for a while afterwards, as we do after a nightmare. If we don't really believe that this is possible, then the danger will encompass us. We have to have some faith that this statement is true, particularly since saints and prophets have recommended it. The best way is to try it with faith and see what happens.

Not only in time of danger, but we can employ this practice, which is called japam in Hinduism, at any time. This repetition of a mantram like OM or a divine name purifies the mind, creates inner calm and peace, and strengthens the spiritual will. It is also a Christian practice. Brother Lawrence in his *Practice of the Presence of God* and the Russian monk in *The Way of the Pilgrim* describe this simple but effective way to calm the mind and be in the presence of the Divine through Its name.

"It is the highest symbol. He who knows it is reverenced as a knower of Brahman." How will we know if a person knows it? Because we are manifestations of Brahman, the OM will reverberate in our minds, and we will know who among us are knowers of the Truth because we are all one.

> The Self, whose symbol is OM, is the omniscient Lord. He is not born. He does not die. He is neither cause nor effect.[50]

The soul is the Atman, is the Self within us; It is never born and never dies. But what about the death we see all around us? Those are deaths to the body, not to the Self.

"He is neither cause nor effect." According to pure Vedanta, the world we see around us, which is an effect, is caused by something that must be like Brahman. This universe couldn't cause itself. That is, by the way, a proof of the existence of God if we need one for the atheist. Look at the Earth. Is it a cause or an effect? It can't be a cause, because it's an effect. And wherever there's an effect, there has to be a cause. Whatever created this, which we may call the Deity or God, the universe is an effect; it may have individual causes flowing out of it, but essentially is an effect.

But here it says, "He is neither cause nor effect." Although He created the universe in a way, He remains apart from it. It's a kind of mirage; it's not real. The world is not permanently real because it changes: Deserts become seas, and oceans become deserts; mountains become valleys, valleys become mountains. We know this has been happening for millions of years and will apparently go on. Therefore this can't be the Supreme, which as St. Paul said, is the same yesterday and today and forever. Everything is changing—the Earth, the moon, the sun and the stars.

The universe is wonderful, but the Spirit is more wonderful—both are wonderful. We must know both; we must go to the Spirit through the world, although holding with one hand to the Spirit as we do, lest we be swallowed up by the divine power in the world. So by holding to meditation, which is the means of holding to the Spirit, we can then live and do everything we're meant to do karmically in the world.

> This Ancient One is unborn, eternal, imperishable; though the body be destroyed, he is not killed.... If the slayer think that he slays, if the slain think that he is slain, neither of them knows the truth. The Self slays not, nor is he slain.[51]

This same idea is also expressed in the *Bhagavad Gita* as noted in Part One. Bodies die; bodies kill; and bodies are killed. The Self doesn't kill, nor is it killed. As long as we

The Problem of Evil

identify with the body, we should resist evil. In that case we can go to war, fight, and perform violent actions against the evil if necessary. As long as we believe (as most do) that some people are enemies, some are no good, we have to fight and even kill from time to time. If we think some things are evil, we have to take action against them. It doesn't do any good to say, "I won't do anything." It's only the mystic or aspiring mystic or saint who doesn't see the evil the way we do, and he or she is not allowed to act. He or she is the one to whom Christ gave the teaching, "resist not evil." But that doesn't apply to the rest of us. The teachings in the Sermon on the Mount are meant for those who want to become saints and mystics. Unfortunately, this was not made clear, so as a result, many of us have had a load of guilt in our lives whenever we've read the Sermon on the Mount thinking these things are meant for us, knowing that we've been unable to carry them out. When Christ said, "resist not evil," he meant this command for someone who doesn't see the evil as evil, as almost all of us do. Buddha and Christ, these great souls, are all-accepting. Brahman is permitting these people to live, so the saints have to do the same.

There are three stages of action regarding evil: In the first stage those who see evil as evil should do what is necessary—fight it, kill it, destroy it, go to war, and so on.

In the middle stage we are not aggressors and we are not saints. We take action, but not violent action. If we took violent action, we would succumb to the evil in ourselves. We have to act like the police officer who restrains and arrests an evil-doer but does it impersonally. This is how we should act: We should restrain an evildoer without killing, because if we kill we will be tainted. The action will taint us; it will degrade us and affect the evildoer as well. But when a soldier and police officer kill in the line of duty, out of necessity, it doesn't degrade them.

In the third, advanced stage, a person recognizes evil in a manner of speaking, but really doesn't see it. He or she sees the Lord's hand in it and doesn't resist. This person won't do anything; he or she may not be a saint, but is close to being a saint. For them and them alone Christ directed the saying, "resist not evil." He was trying to make saints. That is the purpose of a Christ and a Buddha—to make saints. Their mystical teachings are for the few, and it is impossible for the rest of us even to understand these teachings, much less carry them out.

> The Self is not known through study of the scriptures, nor through subtlety of the intellect, nor through much learning; but by him who longs for him is he known. Verily unto him does the Self reveal his true being. [52]

Imagine this quintessential scripture telling us that the Self cannot be known through the study of scriptures. But it must

Scriptural Studies Inadequate

tell the truth that the scriptures cannot lead us to the Deity: They can only prime the mind to get us in the mood, to get us in a state of being conditioned for it. So learning, including theology, philosophy, education and all those things, doesn't lead us toward the Self or toward Self-realization but merely conditions the intellect to enter this world of mystical thought. Who, then, can realize the Self? "By him who longs for him is he known. Unto him does the Self reveal his true being." But the longing for God is such a rare state that most mystics believe this longing is produced by grace. So when the Divine in us stirs, we wonder where this experience is coming from and where it is leading to. We yearn for the source of this extraordinary presence. How can we long for it with our usual dry, arid, intellectual state? We can't; it has to stir in us before we can long for it. So by him who longs for it is He known and yet the longing itself is really produced by the Self wherever a life or a mind is capable of absorbing this inspiration, as we noted earlier in the *Swetasvatara Upanishad*.

By learning a man cannot know him, if he desist not from evil, if he control not his senses, if he quiet not his mind, and practice not meditation.[53]

This statement, in a nutshell, shows the various aspects of the spiritual path. "Desist not from evil," means it is necessary to desist from egotism, and self-centeredness—we have to purge ourselves from all those tendencies. "Control the senses" by practicing nonattachment, since attachments are equal to any kind of evil. When the senses have control over the mind, we get attached to whatever the senses dictate. "If he quiet not his mind"—the mind must be quieted first in order to master the ego and the senses; this is done especially through right meditation. Notice that meditation is at the end of the list, even though it is at the heart of where all these other beneficial results will come from.

Know that the Self is the rider, and the body the chariot; that the intellect is the charioteer, and the mind the reins. The senses, say the wise, are the horses; the roads they travel are the mazes of desire. The wise call the Self the enjoyer when he is united with the body, the senses and the mind.[54]

We can see the richness of this famous metaphor of the chariot and the passenger. It is full of possibilities that we have touched on before. Here we will briefly

The Self as Rider

discuss it and let the student of these scriptures ponder it and discover his or her own interpretations.

The Self is you in your true nature riding through life in the chariot of the body with your intellect or understanding guiding the chariot, and the mind or the will holding the reins together and controlling the horses that represent the five senses.

When a man lacks discrimination and his mind is un-
controlled, his senses are unmanageable, like the restive
horses of a charioteer. But when a man has discrimination
and his mind is controlled, his senses, like the well-broken
horses of a charioteer, lightly obey the rein.[55]

"But when a man has discrimination and his mind is controlled, his senses, like the well-broken horses of a charioteer, lightly
obey the rein." This is a beautiful metaphor of how things should
be. We can easily imagine a different scenario, with the chariot
at the top of a hill ready to descend. The horses are champing at
the bit; the charioteer, the understanding, and the rider are hoping
for a successful journey. We can see that if the charioteer loses
control of the reins, with the horses (senses) champing to go
ahead and run in all directions, the horses will wreck everything.
So we have to hold onto the reins and gently and intelligently
lead the chariot and the horses down the hill.

The Self-Existent made the senses turn outward. Accordingly, man looks toward what is without and sees not
what is within. Rare is he who, longing for immortality,
shuts his eyes to what is without and beholds the Self.[56]

"The Self-Existent made the senses turn outward"—what a
dreadful sentence to ponder. The Self-Existent is the Deity, who

The Senses Turned Outward

could have turned the current of the mind inward but for some reason turned it outward.
It's a dreadful statement because with that act
alone we've been cast out of Eden, so to speak. We might ask
why the Supreme did that. Apparently that is what It wants. As
a result, we believe that the world outside us is real. We never
turn inward unless we are very fortunate, very evolved, or very

desperate. For the most part we look out; we believe everything is without.

"Accordingly, man looks toward what is without and sees not what is within." Supposing the senses and the mind's current had been turned inward, what would happen then? We would see the world around us and say, "Well, it's all changing. It's all right, but I've seen something within me much greater than all these stars and planets and this beautiful earth. It is beautiful but it's nothing: it's here and then it's just gone, but I sense something that won't go. I want to spend my time on that which is permanent." This is what the mystic does—but if we all did this, there would be no propagation of the species. Instead, we would all be contemplators on the Eternal. It would be wonderful in a way—all would be peaceful, tranquil. We would have wonderful lives, but there would be no evolution, no discoveries. We would be like gods or angels, but not exactly saints. Saints are made to struggle through adversity, through conflict, and as a result they know everything. The saint comes out at the end completely changed. Whereas, we wouldn't be changed; we would be like Adam and Eve in the Garden before the fall—beautiful in a way, but limited. The saint is much greater than Adam or Eve because he or she has gone through the whole universe and come out far beyond what they were. Apparently this is the objective of having the senses turned outward and causing us to believe in the reality of the physical, the sense world for many lifetimes.

We can see that we would be insulting the Supreme by turning away from this world too quickly, before we're ready. We have to give It credit, because the world is fascinating. But slowly we realize that it's not getting us anywhere. At some point we seem to be getting into enough trouble that we start to look somewhere else for our answers instead of the outer world. Once we've gone through this stage, we finally turn inward. This begins a whole new sequence that lasts a very long time, too. At the end, the saint has gone through and experienced the whole universe and the whole spiritual realm. And the Deity says, "Now, I have a finished product; now I have someone to commune with; now I have an equal," in a manner of speaking.

> Rare is he who, longing for immortality, shuts his eyes to what is without and beholds the Self.

As long as we look without, we will be mortal. We will have to be reborn over and over again, because the world outside is a world of change and causation, of constant birth and death. If we believe in the reality of the outer world, then we will belong to it. Wherever we put our identification, that's what we belong to. For instance, if we believe in the values of society and conform to them, we will die and we will have to be born over and over again. This society is just nature in a special form; it's changing all the time. But a man "... longing for immortality, shuts his eyes to what is without and beholds the Self." So when we are ready for immortality we turn away from the outer world—but not all at once and not violently because we have to do it gingerly due to the hold of the outer world. We don't want any recoil. Even when we are ready to renounce, it's better to do it slowly but steadily, meanwhile turning within.

> He through whom man experiences the sleeping or waking states is the all-pervading Self. Knowing him, one grieves no more. [57]

If by knowing the Self, one grieves no more, then it follows that not knowing the Truth brings grief. The mystic sees the **The State of Grief** problem in life as a lack of knowing the Truth or the Self, as it's called here. Being ignorant of the Truth, naturally we're in a state of deep sorrow, or grief as Buddha and the Upanishads call it. Not only are we in a state of grief or sorrow, but we don't know that we are, which compounds the problem. Kierkegaard, the famous Danish philosopher of the 19th century, discovered this insight but used the word *despair* instead of *grief*. He said that Man is in a state of despair and the worst part of it is he doesn't know he is. This was a pivotal philosophical moment in history, but Kierkegaard's idea was anticipated by the Vedanta philosophy. Kierkegaard's famous insight showed his deep existential perception, and yet this is a self-evident assumption throughout the Upanishads. In the *Katha Upanishad* we have one of many, many references to it.

We may wonder though, "What state of grief? I'm not grieving." But the Upanishads tell us we are grieving because we are in a state of ignorance, but don't know it. We're like people in prison who don't know they are in prison. The only way they can dream of getting out is, first of all, to know that they are in prison; then they may take steps to find their way out. That's what we are doing in spiritual life. We have found that life, as we know it, is a prison. Now we are in the process of trying to find the escape route. It's not only an escape from something, but also an escape into something—into an enlightened consciousness and new identity.

In the *Chandogya Upanishad* we find a similar statement: "There is no joy in the finite. Only in the Infinite is there joy." [58] If we're looking for joy we can only find it by knowing the Self, or the Infinite—another shocking thought.

Most people feel that life is good, that God created everything for us here in abundance. But the mystic takes the opposite view: We are in a prison, and not knowing that we are prisoners, the misery is deep and enfolds us. Without the mystic's perception we do our best with our social rearrangement, and try to remove things like illiteracy and poverty, but it doesn't seem to remove the Misery Quotient. No matter how we try to juggle things around to alleviate these problems in society, we still end up with the same amount.

If, according to the truth of the Upanishads, we are souls but don't know that we are, we are in a state of sorrow. We may hide the sorrow in many ways, but underneath there will be a deep state of grief. If we are not souls, then the works that reformers and others are performing are the right course of action. Ultimately, by removing suffering and making enough changes, we will get satisfaction and perhaps happiness. But if the mystics are right, then, although those changes are not wrong, they can't remove the misery or the sorrow, which is removable only by knowing the Truth. The Upanishads assume this and never explain, defend, or elaborate on this statement. In the midst of this description of the Self, the sage casually mentions, "Knowing him, one grieves no more." As though this is self-evident, he doesn't even continue this theme but leaves it to go on with what he was saying before. "Grieving no more" is a mere corollary of this problem of the Self and Maya, or untruth.

We aren't aware of this state of misery because we hide it from each other through many ways—some of them socially acceptable, and some of them not. This sorrow and discontent that animates human life is not only among the poor, uneducated and the ill, but everybody. The mystic sees the whole thing in another light entirely, different even from how educated people see the world. We have to decide who is right.

This kind of subject lends itself to reason, analysis, and reflection. One of the limbs of yoga, jnana yoga, is this kind of study that stretches the mind. Even though **Reason vs. Intuition** reason won't bring us directly to realization, we should try to penetrate this enigma by way of reason as much as we can. Having done that, from time to time, we get intuitive flashes of the Truth. We look at our friends, family, coworkers, and suddenly we see them in a new light. It's as though there is a kind of conspiracy of silence to act as if everything is all right.

Although reason and intuition seem to be different, they are still connected by mental processes. It's like a blanket that is smooth on one side and rough on the other side—it's a different texture, but still the same blanket. So here, it's still the same mind, with reason functioning differently from intuition. Reason is more limited; it hobbles along. We have to stretch the mind as much as we can in our attempts to analyze our way to the Truth. This exercises the whole mind, and when reason seems to flag or withdraw, we discover that this conditions the intuitive area to send up its insights. Whereas, if we didn't analyze at all, the intuitions are more creaturely, more simple, and more like the kind that everybody has. Spiritual intuition seems to depend not only on divine grace but on stretching the mind towards spiritual perception as much as possible.

TIME VS. ETERNITY

He who knows that the individual soul, enjoyer of the fruits of action, is the Self—ever present within, lord of time, past and future—casts out all fear.[59]

Lord of time—notice this idea dropped in as though it's very significant, which it is. Meister Eckhart said that time is one of the chief evils of life; by that he meant the consciousness of time. So here the Self is the lord of time because whatever is unlike the Deity is unreal and a source of misery. The Deity is beyond time— timeless—and according to Isaiah in the Bible, the Holy One that inhabits eternity. Eternity is not out in space, a science-fiction world, but is right here, wherever we are—it's not a matter of place but a state of timelessness. When we are at our best, like when our meditation is particularly good, we don't have a sense of time, we have only the present moment in which we are trying to fulfill ourselves and discover its essence, and the past or future doesn't bother us or draw us out much.

Only the present, the "eternal now" is real, consequently, the moment we think of the past or future, we are not grounded in the Real. But because we spend so much of our mental time on the past and the future, they become our main realities. The present seems to be here only for us to worry about the past and project into the future. But in meditation we reverse that, as we reverse everything. In meditation we make the present moment the reality and try not to let the past or the future draw us out. Unfortunately, they do, but we struggle against them and gradually we succeed in being in the present moment. If we could succeed in living in the present all the time, we wouldn't need any other discipline; this alone would be enough.

Leading the spiritual life takes all our attention. We have so many other things to do; we have responsibilities such as raising
The Challenge of Spiritual Life
a family, having a job, dealing with difficult people, keeping ourselves healthy, and all those things that use up our time and attention, and we're asked to think of the spiritual too. Naturally, we will have lapses, periods of forgetfulness. Spiritual life is like a gathering of forces, it takes a long time to mobilize ourselves to be able to live it and at the same time do all these other things.

How are we going to apply these lessons of truth in our life, when we're constantly forgetting them? It's assumed that we will need a lot of time to build up a foundation so that we can begin to practice the truth when we are not meditating. Even when we meditate it's hard enough to keep the mind from disturbing us with its habits and so on. Six months or a year is nothing in spiritual life, though it sounds like a lot because you can usually do a lot of things in a year. But here that's just a beginning; it takes a few years to get a taste of it and apply these ideas.

Time means nature, change. Time means the body, the mind, cause and effect. Time represents all those things that the Deity is not. The Deity is beyond change, beyond nature, beyond body and mind, beyond cause-and-effect, and so on. So time is unknown to the mind of the Deity, unknown to the Self, and unknown to a Buddha or a Christ. The avatar knows our world the way we know the world of children: We know most of what they're going through, but it has no reality to us anymore. It's just an idea, whereas the children are immersed in that reality.

We remember enough of it to be able to relate to them. Similarly, the great mystic remembers enough of these other concepts to be able to relate to others and know what they are going through. We see children suffering about things that are not worth their time. We usually know what is bothering them and we can take steps to alleviate it or remove it. So the great mystic knows what is bothering us in the same way. Ramakrishna said that the enlightened soul looks on everyone in the world as his or her children. These spiritual masters look on the entire world's passions literally as children's passions. They don't regard them as worth the trouble that we give them, in the same way that we have been through children's passions and we know that they aren't worth troubling over, but we, like the children, don't know that.

The illumined soul sympathizes with us up to a point; he or she can't get into it too much because it's an unreal world that is causing so much sorrow. As with children, we feel for them but at the same time we are detached even as we are compassionate. So this is the way the liberated soul is with humanity. Compassion is certainly there, but it's mixed with an equal degree of reserve. Otherwise, it would be like the Lord sorrowing with us when we sorrow—the Lord is beyond our sorrows, as we are when we come to our senses. When that happens, where's the sorrow? It was unreal, like a cloud. Inhabiting eternity the Lord cannot realize the things of time; inhabiting the Truth, clothed with Truth, He cannot know the things of untruth.

These great ones are compassionate with us, as we are with the younger ones behind us. We wish we could help them; we think about them and pray for them. The worst part is that we know it's all unnecessary, but they don't know this. They don't have perspective, or understanding that is given to us through time and struggle. If we could give them our understanding of their problem, they would see it in a new light and be free from it. So it is with us; all we have to do is see ourselves and our problems in this new light and that will free us. That's what we're trying to do in spiritual life.

The child or adolescent is grieving most of the time. Lacking perspective, he's filled with himself, and not only himself but an unreal conception of himself. So he grieves because of ignorance and a lack of understanding, not because someone else hurt him, or she stood him up, or they won't let him on the football team and life is not worth living. If we could give them our understanding they would be free from their grief.

As we grow out of those adolescent agonies, we replace them with other ones. The worst agony of all is the agony of life itself — not adolescence, not childhood, but life. In adulthood, we have all our powers and still cannot discover why we are living or what we are here for or who we are. But the grief and the sorrow are for the same reason as with the adolescent: We lack understanding. If we see ourselves and our problems in a true light, then we jump out of that false state quickly and wonder how we could have believed in it all those years.

AS WITHIN, SO WITHOUT

> What is within is also without. What is without is also within. He who sees difference between what is within and what is without goes evermore from death to death.[60]

"What is within is also without. What is without is also within." Chiefly this means that the Self is within us; we are not separate from the Self, and the Self is also without. It isn't as though the Self is a witness to all the eternal things like love, life, and joy. The Self is the love, the joy, the existence — this is the Self's nature. These are merely names whereby the intellect defines it for its own purpose.

The Self is within; Life is within. Each of us is a carrier of the whole life of the universe. The Upanishads started with this ultimate statement at the dawn of religious history. Even now we stagger towards the idea as though it's the latest revelation. This bold statement is very modern and overwhelming in its implications. But in almost every paragraph of the Upanishads, set down over 2,500 years ago, this is their first and last word. They never developed or explained it. *He who has ears to hear, let him hear.* We are told that we are carriers of the whole life of the universe within us. And we want to settle for just a little mortal, finite existence. But it's hard to shake off the trammels of this old consciousness that makes us believe in a limited, separate existence. We need to hear and reflect on these ideas so that we can slowly move towards a more concrete awareness of the reality of the Self.

"What is without is also within." The Self is everywhere. So when we see other people, we must be careful not to hate them or harm them because the Self is equally in them as it is in us. This brings us back to Christ's statement: "Resist not evil." We see how Vedanta throws light on this difficult, mysterious saying of Christ. There's no real evil from the point of view of the Self. The evil exists in terms of human beings who have been conditioned in one way or another, but to the Self everything has a purpose and is allowed to exist. We can't say that anything that is permitted to exist is evil exactly; it may have a negative, rough function or catalytic function, which in terms of evolution might be called evil, but in terms of mysticism, or the Self, it's not evil.

If you are a practicing mystic, you must be careful to overcome evil with good and love your enemies, as Christ said. Who can really love their enemies except the mystic, and near-saint? But Christ wants us to be perfect. The rest of us can't love our enemies, but at best we tolerate them, are civil towards them, and with much effort we can accept them. That's about as far as we can go, but it's better than hating them. It is a long way from where we used to be when we thought the solution was an eye for an eye, and a tooth for a tooth—the old law—that's not Christ's law or the Upanishadic law, but the law of mankind, of states, of governments. Christ's law says that you must love these people. Why should we love others who are hateful, who are our enemies? Because the Self is in them, even though they may not know it. They may not be acting well, but that does not change their inherent reality. The Self has created them and permitted them to live; It has accepted them. Therefore, if you are a mystic, you have to accept them. If you want to have the Self accept you, you have to accept the creation in totality, not in part.

We wonder what Christ means in the Sermon on the Mount:

Do unto others, as you would have them do unto you. (Matthew 7: 12)

Love your enemies … do good to them that hate you. (Matthew 5: 44)

The kingdom of heaven is within you. (Matthew 7:12)

We don't really know what he meant, but we can still believe—and that's usually the best we can do. But the Upanishads throw light on the meaning of these passages. It's self-evident what Christ meant: He knew the Self within is also the Self without.

> He who sees difference between what is within and what is without goes ever more from [life to life and] death to death.

By seeing differences we believe in the world of change, of opposites, of life and death, good and evil, and so on. We forget that we are one with Brahman and this constitutes our ignorance, which ensures that we will be born over and over again.

> As rain, fallen on a hill, streams down its side, so runs he after many births who sees manifoldness in the Self.[61]

To reinforce this idea we are given another powerful image showing the inevitability of karmic rebirth the way rain streams down a hill—with the momentum of gravity behind it, nothing can prevent this. Similarly, when people see differences between themselves and others, there's no way they can be stopped from this round of births and deaths and the attendant suffering. When rain streams down a hillside, it does so compulsively; it has to. Similarly, we become what we see: If we see multiplicity outside, we will have many lives to live. Whatever we see, we become. If we see all these differences instead of oneness, then we won't have the One.

Not only that, but as the rain streams down a hill, it falls into a kind of nothingness. We don't know what happens to the water. So the image is twofold: The rain flowing irresistibly down a hillside suggests the compulsiveness of our rebirths, and the way the water dissipates and seems to end nowhere implies that we end nowhere as well. If we act simply as human beings—judging,

finding complexity, multiplicity, and manifoldness in the One—
we end nowhere; we are scattered. As T. S. Eliot wrote:

> This is the way the world ends
> Not with a bang, but a whimper.

We just whimper down into a state of nothingness. That is how
each individual life will end until we can do better.

FROM THE "Self" TO THE "Self"

> As pure water poured into pure water remains pure, so
> does the Self remain pure, O Nachiketa, uniting with
> Brahman.[62]

In the act of uniting with Brahman what was the *self* becomes
the capitalized *Self*. In the mystical climax the individual self
becomes the Self and reveals Its true nature. The stillness of the
Self needs to be approximated before we can experience It. It
usually takes some time before the mind is properly tempered.

We have to resemble that which we are going to experience.
In human terms, if we want to experience love, we have to be
loving. If we want to retain love we have to continue to be loving;
it isn't only at the beginning that we love and then forever
afterwards expect to be loved as we are. More often than not, in
marriages the problem is that we don't continue to act as we did
in the beginning. There's a law here: We have to be loving in
order to earn the love. When we aren't loving and the love doesn't
come to us, we tend to blame the other person, as though we can
violate the law and get away with it. Most of us don't know there's
a law here, but the spiritual person begins to know these things,
and if married, he or she can apply these priceless insights into

married life or any close relationship. Even apart from that, with our relations to humanity as a whole, people will respond to us as we do to them.

"As pure water poured into pure water remains pure, so does the Self remain pure." This scripture says that we are always pure, and since purity is an absolute thing, we can't develop into it, we can't work into it: We can only remove the impurities that have covered it. The impurities are accidents of karma, the habits we pick up. The scum of habits overlays the pure water, but the beautiful pure water itself is unchanged by the stagnation on top of it. This in summary is the Vedantic concept: The stagnant growth of our ignorant lives has covered the pure water of our true nature; through our spiritual practice and spiritual discriminations, we gradually winnow away this rank vegetative growth. All we do is remove the impurities; we don't attain anything.

This is also the Yoga ideal, which gets most of its emphasis from the Vedantic scriptures. The yogi says the same thing; what we do is remove the bad habits, the Maya in the mind through disciplined concentration, analysis, nonattachment, and so on, until finally the distractions get less and less and the mind grows quieter. If we go on this way sufficiently, one day the mind says, "Eureka!" Suddenly something shines in the mind. It's like the lake in the mountain that is covered over with rank scum, but by removing the debris, at a certain point we can see the sun shining, reflected perfectly on the still, calm surface of the lake.

This is in contrast with the Christian concept that believes we attain, accomplish, and reach the goal—a psychology embedded in our Western minds particularly because of our active natures. In the West, we like the idea of reaching and accomplishing, scaling mountains, crossing oceans, and reaching the other shore. This is all right because we have to be active, but it becomes tiring—we are striving and swimming, and the shore is ever receding for what seems like a long time. But in the Vedantic view, we take our stand on the indwelling Presence that we carry around with us all the time, like a perfume, and winnow away the obstacles instead of striving to reach something that is distant. In the Christian view, as sinners, we must be distant from the Divine, and therefore strive towards some mysterious, ever-receding shore. If we are Christian or Muslim and are fortunate enough to reach the shore, we discover: "Lo and behold, the shore is me! It was in me all the time." We may not acknowledge it in those terms because of our upbringing, but Meister Eckhart and a few others have reached the shore and announced, "The shore is me, it's in me, and everything is in me!" Jesus also says, "The kingdom of heaven is within you"—the same Vedantic emphasis. This approach is less tiring and more realistic.

According to Eckhart, the Divine is seeking to be born in the form of the Divine Son every moment, every second. And according to Vedanta, and Ramakrishna, divine grace is pouring through us every minute. So we don't have to do all the work. Our job then is to remove the obstacles, since the Self, the Divine cannot do that. Why would we expect the Divine to do that? Things that we have clearly caused are our problem, so that whatever we can do, the Deity won't do. It's what we can't do that It does, such as bring about realization. The Divine is the secret doer, the secret power—both the Yoga and Vedanta philosophies take their stand on this premise.

So pure water, in the first instance here is the individual self in its true nature, when poured into the pure water of Brahman remains pure. This is a very encouraging reminder that we are not sinners seeking somehow to be saved but rather we are an unknown purity seeking to merge with the Unknown Purity. This is the emphasis of Vedanta. True, we have a lot of work to do— but we can do it in that context rather than the context of being sinners. How can a sinner unite with sinlessness? If sinlessness is an absolute condition, the sinner's nature can't be changed into sinlessness. It's like changing fire into water. Fire is destined to remain fire, and water to remain water. So Purity is purity. And if it's purity at a certain point of realization, as it will have to be to merge with the Supreme Purity, it always was that, even though not known to itself.

THE SELF IN EVERYTHING

Near the end of the *Katha Upanishad* there are a series of brilliant images using fire, air, and the sun to express the same idea. For example:

> As air, though one, takes the shape of every object in which it enters, so the Self, though one, takes the shape of every object in which it dwells.[63]

So for everyone you see, the Self has assumed that form. This is the mystic view; it is also Jesus' teaching. That is why we are to love others, accept them, do good to them, and serve them. *Love your neighbor as yourself.* What did Jesus mean by that? Your neighbor *is* yourself. This philosophy makes clear what Christ meant. There's only one Self, one humanity, one life. The thing that gets in the way is the apparent multiplicity of forms, as we noted earlier. The forms are many, but the forms are not the reality. The reality is what tenants the forms, what inhabits the forms. This is where we make the mistake: We judge the forms as real because the forms are undoubtedly many, but the Self in them, the One in them is not many. That is where we have to make a distinction.

We can't all be beautiful. If everyone were beautiful, it would be kind of monotonous. Beauty is wonderful because of its rarity. If everyone were beautiful, we wouldn't prize beauty so much. So ugliness is necessary for contrast. In fact, if there was only one ugly person in a town of beautiful people, that person would be the most attractive because everyone would want to see him or her—it would be such a relief. We might even see the criminal, the person acting badly in a similar light because he doesn't know any better. It's like he's mentally handicapped. We see mentally handicapped people and they're kind of bad actors, they shout, break things, and giggle—but somehow we understand them. If you understand a person enough you can forgive them anything. So we forgive the mentally disabled person, no matter what they do because they don't always know what they're doing. It's irresponsible behavior, like what a child would do. We can't judge the child, and so it is with the mentally handicapped person. What about evildoers, who are not children, and do not have delayed development? Well, the mystic says they *are* children, they are developmentally retarded in a way. The wicked are the same to the mystic, and to a Christ. So when these "children" get together and put him on the cross and kill him, he says, "Father, forgive them for they know not what they do." We feel bitter, but he says they are like children or mentally handicapped.

The air takes the shape of every object it enters, and the Self takes the shape of every object in which it dwells. We have to try to remember that with the help of meditation.

Brahman words cannot reveal, mind cannot reach, eyes
cannot see. How then, save through those who know him,
can he be known?[64]

"Brahman words cannot reveal, mind cannot reach, eyes
cannot see" — we have to go beyond the mind. Although we have
to work within the mind at first, in meditation we gradually start
to go where we ultimately will go: beyond the mind.

"How then, save through those who know him, can he be
known?" Only the person who knows Brahman can convey the
conviction, the message, and the reality of the truth of Brahman,
as well as the way, the path, to reach Brahman. How except
through such can Brahman be known? This is an integral part of
the Hindu tradition, the idea of the knower of Brahman or the
sage figure as guru, who is necessary to transmit these teachings.

THE UPANISHADS – THE ULTIMATE TEACHING

Wherever they take us, the Upanishads always come back to the
same center. They never lose sight of what they are doing even in
the midst of many interesting illustrations. The illustrations,
beautiful and priceless though they are, are just discourse, just
words; but the reality behind them is that which brings the mind
of the discourser, the mind of the speaker or student, back over
and over again to the central theme no matter how brilliant the
illustration. Other philosophers and poets have their rich
illustrations, comparisons, contrasts, and explanations that
fascinate us and can take us away for pages and pages. Oftentimes
we don't get back to the center because, with them, they started

with words and they continue with words, whereas the rishis start with Reality and the words pay homage to that Truth.

So we find the central message that we keep coming back to over and over again in the *Katha Upanishad*, as in all the Upanishads: The Self is all, and you are the Self. To overcome death and become immortal, you must realize your true identity, realize your oneness with all life by knowing the Self, and then you will be free from the wheel of birth and death.

This is the secret teaching. If we are not ready for the ideas of the Upanishads, it will remain a secret to us—but if we are ready, it is the ultimate teaching.

PART THREE

Brahman

Ralph Waldo Emerson, the great American essayist and Transcendentalist, was one of the first in America to study and recognize the value of the scriptures of the Orient. During his time, he made these teachings known through his writings and thereby influenced many others, notably Walt Whitman and Henry David Thoreau, whose own classics continue to be a source of inspiration to many.

In this section, Emerson's poem "Brahma" is used as a starting point to illustrate and expand on the concept of "Brahman."

10

⚘ Emerson's "Brahma"

Brahman, filling the Upanishads, is the great word in Hinduism. It stands for the Supreme Being, the Absolute. Ralph Waldo Emerson captured the essence of the concept in his famous poem, "Brahma."[65]

> If the red slayer think he slays;
>   Or if the slain think he is slain;
> They know not well the subtle ways;
>   I keep, and pass, and turn again.
>
> Far or forgot to me is near;
>   Shadow and sunlight are the same;
> The vanished gods to me appear;
>   And one to me are shame and fame.
>
> They reckon ill who leave me out;
>   When me they fly, I am the wings;
> I am the doubter and the doubt,
>   And I the hymn the Brahmin sings.
>
> The strong gods pine for my abode,
>   And pine in vain the sacred Seven;
> But thou, meek lover of the good!
>   Find me, and turn thy back on heaven.

Brahman is the Doer. Brahman has become everything.

All is Brahman   Brahman is the power that does not stand outside the world, but becomes the world and yet transcends it. This is pantheism—with a difference. The pantheist goes out into the country and says, "God has become all this: trees, lakes, mountains, tigers, lambs, and so forth." *Pantheism* means "the deity in all." But Brahman is also much more. Pantheism omits the fact that the world is only a portion of the Deity, of Brahman. Just as we don't think that a man consists of his body primarily, but of something much more, so the body of God—the mountains and so on—is only a small fraction of Its totality. The pantheist tends to overlook the spiritual reality that is embodied *partially* in the world of Nature. Therefore, God has become all this—not only Nature, but the whole universe. Brahman, however, is a transcendental reality. It not only is immanently present in the world, and the omnipresent spirit, but It is also transcendent to that world. It's both simultaneously. This is a colossal concept. Brahman is the power behind everything. "If the slayer think he slays,/ Or if the slain think he is slain...." It does everything. Although we think we are the doer, It is.

> Far or forgot to me is near;
>   Shadow and sunlight are the same;
> The vanished gods to me appear;
>   And one to me are shame and fame.

I, Brahman, am the Doer. Time does not exist for Me, nor space, nor darkness, nor light. Darkness is part of My being; light is part of My being. Light is closer to My essence, just as good is closer to My essence than evil, but I am beyond both. Evil is necessary for My creation. Violence and death are necessary for My creation.

We can't have just life; we must have death, to make it go on. We can't have just lambs, but tigers—and so forth. We must have opposition. Why? Why should it be that way? We don't know exactly. Sometimes we are confronted with a mystery. Why should the world exist at all? The question—as Buddha would say—is not edifying. Questions like this do not help us, even though we have to ask them for a while. We see that there is no end to them. Why did it start in the first place? We cannot answer that kind of question—those who could, have never given us an answer.

The Upanishads suggest that at some point there was Brahman alone—or the Self alone as it is sometimes called, the Self of all. This isn't the ordinary self, which is the ignorant or limited self, the one that we work with in order to infuse it, sublimate it, and irradiate it with *This,* which is within; it is the Self that is Brahman.

"The vanished gods to me appear." Gods, religions, civilizations come and go. Brahman remains, the support of it all.

"And one to me are shame and fame." To us, in these pairs of opposites—good and evil, shame and fame, and so forth—one is good, and one is not good. But to Brahman they are all good. As we've seen in the *Katha Upanishad,* everything that exists has a necessary existence. Therefore, the mystic finds, it is good.

We tend to forget Brahman, this impersonal Reality: "They reckon ill who leave me out." We fly from it: "Though I take the wings of the morning and fly to the uttermost parts of the sea, even there shall thy hand lead me."[66] The Hindu would add that Brahman is also the wings that you've taken: "When me they fly, I am the wings." It is a strange doctrine.

Christ, praying to the Father in Heaven, says: "Lead us not into temptation, but deliver us from evil." By this statement he seems to imply that God is the power that leads us into temptation. According to the Hindus, Brahman is behind the temptation itself. And Christ seems to confirm that by implication. This phrase in the Lord's Prayer has puzzled many people. But the Upanishads throw light on it. It may not make it more welcome to us, but it does help to explain it: the Deity pervades everything, including temptation; and It also pervades that in us which is led into temptation.

Where are we then? We seem helpless. Are we caught up in a cycle of determinism? Are we simply chips on this wave that is really doing everything?

Brahman is also the power in us that can renounce the world and conquer the lower self. This is particularly known as the Shiva-power—Shiva being the Hindu god representing destruction and renunciation. (The other two gods in the Hindu triumvirate are Vishnu, who protects and sustains the world, and Brahma, the creator. These are the three aspects of the Personal God, Ishvara or Brahman when it is involved in creation.) It is just like a play, then—a divine play—in which one part of the Godhead is pitted against another. So God may lead us into temptation, may provide the temptation, and may even say, "If you want to destroy yourself, go ahead—and here is the energy for destruction." There's always the caveat, however, that you have to come back and do it all over again. Brahman provides all that *and* the willpower and the spiritual exercises to overcome all of it and lead us out of the temptation. So although temptation is real and the impulse to yield to temptation is real, the power within us to resist it is also real. And it is the very power of that temptation that calls forth this greater power to resist it.

Through temptation we find out what we are capable of. If we get past the temptation, we get stronger; the power of the temptation passes into us as we overcome it. But if we fail and succumb to the temptation, we also gain. How can we gain when we lose? We learn from the experience and we become humble. A certain amount of failures are necessary. But if we put ourselves in situations where we will be tempted, thinking we can handle them, there's a risk of playing God. In that case the price to pay will be humiliation and bad experiences. Therefore, whenever possible, we should avoid situations where there is temptation; then we will be safe from the consequences of this extreme subtlety.

Even within the Godhead there are evidently modifications. Some things are said to lie closer to Pure Being than others; they are closer to the center of the circle. For instance, good lies closer to it than evil, because when we're doing evil things we're not aware of any unity, harmony, Godhead, or any other reality: We're aware only of their opposites and are moving farther away from the center. When we have good thoughts and are doing good actions without seeking any reward, we have a feeling of strength, unity, cohesion, substance, reality—a sense of *being real.* We are moving closer to the center. In that respect, good lies closer to the center—but it is *not* the center, as we know from many well-meaning, ethical people who have not realized Brahman. They are far from realization, yet they are much closer to the center than those who give in to their disruptive, egoistic motives and live for the day, for the ego-self. This we must not do. If we do, we will give in to that part of us that takes us farther and farther out to the periphery of things, where we have no contact with our true identity. We have to discipline the lower self and strengthen the higher through spiritual exercises. This doesn't require necessarily leading a monastic life, or a life of Spartan renunciation, but we need *some* sort of discipline, *some* inner check every day. Then we begin to feel another power growing in us— *that* is the true Brahman. And the force in us that wants to say, "Be done with it, just live for the day," is the ephemeral self, which along with the body and senses has an impermanent, mortal existence.

Well, what's the point of all this? It seems just like a merry-go-round. We are led into temptation; we're led out of it. In the **Brahman's Mirror** process, we become mirrors of Brahman, which does not know Itself. It knows everything in the universe, but not Itself. Perhaps, then, this play that goes on, this dream, this struggle of opposites, this war of contraries within the being of the Godhead is the way by which the Godhead can discover what It is. It is the eternal subject, but not the object of anything. Everything in the universe is the object; It is the subject. It is the knower; everything else is known. It never knows Itself. As Yagnavalkya asked in the *Brihadaranyaka Upanishad*: "By whom shall the Knower be known?" Who is to know Brahman? What mind is there that could use Brahman as an object for knowledge and understanding? It would have to be something greater than Brahman, which is the irreducible Absolute. Brahman knows everything else, but not Itself—unless it becomes a mirror of Itself.

You never see your own face, except through reflection. Suppose there were no mirrors in the world, no reflective surfaces. How would you ever know what you looked like, or what you were? You would have to find your reflection in your relationships, in people, in other faces, and gradually you would discern what and who you are. We have become a mirror for Brahman, and so this terrible struggle, this agony that humanity goes through, and then the individual aspirant goes through in a new and deliberate way, is part of the necessary process whereby we discover the truth of who we are, and present a mirror for this Infinite Being to realize Itself. Otherwise without this struggle, the Godhead would never know what it is. Meister Eckhart, the boldest of the Western thinkers, said that God would not know that He existed if it weren't for him: He enables God to know that He exists. But Eckhart was a mystic of the highest order. If we said the same thing, it would be like a baby's meaningless prattle. We might say, "I enable God to know himself," but we know that's nonsense. In our case, the "I" that is speaking is just a baby, an unrealized self. It is like the self of animals, of plants, a mere natural identity.

The "I" that Eckhart was referring to is the consciousness in him that realized the Truth, that realized Itself. This is the same "I" that Christ referred to when he said, "I am the Way, the Truth, and the Life." And when someone asked Buddha, "What are you?" He said, "I am awake—I am the Awakened." The "I" that responded to this question was not the "I" in the ordinary man that had questioned him. It was the "I" of the Self—the awakened consciousness, the "I" of Self-realization. When this dormant consciousness, the Atman, awakens within us, it becomes the Truth, the mystical consciousness.

What has all that got to do with Brahman? That *is* Brahman.

Nirvana   That *is* Nirvana. These are all names for the same thing. As already noted, Nirvana means *extinguishing,* and Westerners have thought it means to extinguish life. No, it means extinguishing that which will prevent *this* (the Self) from knowing itself as *That* (Brahman). Nirvana is the unitive state in which false egoism and false desire are extinguished. After the extinction of the false life and individuality, we discover Nirvana while still in the body. Nirvana may come after death, but there is no recommendation to seek it there. Nirvana is part of our being. Nirvana *is* our being. In reality, we are Nirvana—but instead we identify with the shadows that pass in front of it and tell ourselves that they are reality.

> They reckon ill who leave me out;
> When me they fly, I am the wings;
> I am the doubter and the doubt....

I am the temptation; I lead you into it; and I am also the deliverance. You might say, "Well, if Brahman will deliver me, what is there for me to do then? Shall I just sit back and be tempted and delivered?" No, that attitude is pointless. Deliverance cannot come without the strength that we call willpower, which is also Brahman. We have all felt this great fire at different times after exerting our will in doing our duties against resistance, or at so many other times when we haven't wanted to do something but did it because we knew we should. It made us feel like new individuals. This strength is an example of the spiritual will, the higher consciousness, imposing itself on the lesser, mere creature-will or self-will that says, "I will not." It is the higher will that says, "I'll do this because I must, and I'm going to conquer the inner resistance to it." We can see the struggle between them. When we do our duty because we know it's the right

Brahman: Tempter and Deliverer

thing to do, even though we don't want to, we feel liberated—to a small measure, admittedly. But every time we win these victories against our lower nature, which we have the opportunity for every day, we get a sample of the spiritual path, a taste of the whole journey.

If we're raising a family, studying for a degree in college, or trying to master any kind of art or science, there's a great deal of willpower involved. So that the best part of education, or of raising a family, is the education of the self—it's not so much mastering knowledge or raising children, as mastering ourselves, raising ourselves. In raising children it is ourselves that we are raising anew, our real self. In mastering an education it is ourselves we are mastering every semester, every paper, every examination. These are merely the pretexts for the real education that's going on. Education here meaning to *draw out* something that is there to *be* drawn out. It is like fire in a firestick. Raising a family draws out something; it changes us. Mastering anything, with all the discipline and sacrifice involved, changes us; it educates us. Education brings out something that is covered in darkness and nonawareness, but is resident there from the beginning. We have conflicts and temptations that we struggle against, and this very struggle itself draws out something. The appearance of this will is the beginning; it is like the spearhead of the emerging Self. The higher will is the first face of the emerging soul, the Atman, that we see.

11

✿ Brahman and the Individual Soul

What is the soul, or the Atman as it is called in Hinduism? Where is it? It is formless, vague. We don't know what it is. It begins to

The Spiritual Seeker

announce its presence in meditation, and in spiritual moods that are foreign to the intellect and of which the intellect has no knowledge. We are puzzled by these moods because we judge our normal everyday experiences to be the truth of our being. When something happens that is foreign to our usual experience we wonder what it means. These are premonitions of the soul's restlessness to be heard, listened to, and turned to—that is, for the mind to be turned in its direction. The soul announces itself in these ways, but they are rather tentative and we are not sure of them. Unless we're already embarked on the spiritual path we tend to ignore them, or perhaps to make poetry out of them the way William Wordsworth did. But we usually don't realize their significance.

The soul more effectively announces itself in terms of morality and moral challenges. This is why morals have always been considered so important. Morality lies close to the area of conscience, of duty, of "ought"—it is an immortal, permanent reality. Sociologists and anthropologists explain morality in terms of environmental mores and the influences that work upon us, and they point out that in different cultures there are different morals and different standards of conscience, therefore there is no permanent reality. We have heard that pervasive argument, but it only concerns the ordinary, phenomenal self—the life we all know. On that level what they say is quite true: There is no such thing as a permanent principle behind conscience or standards of morality in the world. From that standpoint, it is true that morals are optional. Every culture determines its moral standards and it imposes those standards on its members. Anthropologists, sociologists, and psychologists have proven this.

But here we are not concerned with this aspect of morality, except that we have to accommodate ourselves to that part of our life. The person who is seeking spiritual realization enters into a different zone of consciousness, of being, where other realities are announced: the realities that have come to sages and mystics down through the centuries in all religions. The spiritual seeker begins a trek up the mountain of spiritual life that most people never undertake; in fact, most people deny that the mountain exists. But when we begin to climb the mountain, even when we are in the foothills, we enter into another world apart from most others. Those who have climbed that mountain before us have had the same experiences that we have, although the names that they use vary. We may say it isn't Brahman we are seeking, but instead God, or Christ, or Buddha. Our background will determine the terms we use. The basic reality of the search— the struggle, insights, hope, thirsts, realizations that gradually come, as well as friendships, the necessity of spiritual association, and the inevitable suffering of change that we go through—is unknown to the worlds of sociology and anthropology. But all spiritual seekers know what the search involves. It is a universal condition.

Along the way we discover new things constantly, and in fact the surges of spiritual thought and emotion that come to us are so powerful that the mind has to be invigorated and the nervous system has to adjust to absorb them. If this doesn't happen, the body and nervous system will be overwhelmed and we will have breakdowns. This often happens to people who rush ahead too quickly in spiritual life, who try to have mystical experiences prematurely, and who resort to various kinds of occult practices or drugs to bring them on. The nervous system, the brain structure, is simply not strong enough yet to absorb these powerful surges of spiritual thinking and emotion, which are like nothing we have had before. We have to have a new structural building, a new body, another nervous system, another network of brain cells and nervous connections between them. Meditation, prayer, contemplation, and spiritual reading gradually change the system so that it can accommodate the emerging consciousness.

We learn what morality really means as we experience a new conscience. We *have* to behave in a certain manner. Other people

Right and Wrong   may have the option to act morally or not, but the spiritual person has no choice and must act rationally and ethically; otherwise the mind will be restless and the foundation of his or her spiritual practices—meditation— will suffer. Successful meditation will be impossible. This is one of the scourges that lashes us into acceptance; but after a while we find that it is not really a scourge after all. We see that in spiritual life morality is not a relative thing, as the anthropologists believe it to be. However, on the societal, cultural level of society there is no such thing as a permanent moral standard in the world. It fluctuates; we've seen it fluctuate even in our time. Therefore, who is to say what's right? That argument is unanswerable. But the spiritual person discovers that there is an absolute right and wrong, and has to abide by what is right or spiritual progress comes to a halt.

An awakening consciousness, mind, outlook, and personality are attained through spiritual living—but gradually, not all at once. Spiritual aspirants discover in the process that the scriptures, which are based on the assumption of a permanent reality, exist to guide them in this endeavor.

According to the worlds of sociology, anthropology, and psychology, there *is* no permanence in this world. "My kingdom is not of this world," says Christ. That's what we say also; it is the cry of the soul. It doesn't mean that we want to escape the world; we accommodate ourselves to it. We live in the world, but our true kingdom is within. We render unto Caesar the things that are Caesar's in order to get him away from us, in order not to be bothered so that we can pursue our true interests. And we render unto God the things that are God's while we are living here, not in heaven, not in another life, which would only be postponing the struggle. We have to do it here. The Vedas say that it can be done on other planes, too; but it is probably better to do it here because there is more opportunity and greater incentive to do so.

The strong gods pine for my abode.

The gods may rule the universe but they cannot find Me, Brahman, because, although great beings, they are still egocentrically motivated. The lord our God is a jealous God: "You must give up all sense of self if you want Me, I am the only Self. *Thou shalt have no other gods before Me.* If you have any other gods, I won't destroy you, you can have them if you want to. If you want heavens, if you want to *be* gods, you can." You can have all that— but it will all wear out in time. Everything comes to an end. Desires reach their fulfillment, and eventually you'll have to return to the starting point. Gods are gods by desire and good karma, according to the Vedas, and hence even they are replaced.

12

The Last Temptation

If you want Brahman, if you want the Truth, you must give up the idea of dominating and ruling others, of attaining esoteric knowledge and exercising occult powers—

Occult Powers

all of this has to be abandoned, although it is indeed hard to do. The desire to have special influence, secret powers, is deep in all of us. It is perhaps the last temptation. It makes dealing with lust, anger, hatred, and greed seem relatively simple, because you can see them for what they are and find some way of fighting them. But spiritual seekers discover occult powers within themselves as they advance toward perfection. We all have this as part of our basic constitution. We are all psychic, occultist in potential. This veiled world of the subconscious contains everything from criminality to genius to sainthood— everything is within. Nothing whatsoever is excluded.

As we travel along on the spiritual path we fight off the grosser temptations like greed, which is pernicious and quite distasteful. We fight off anger, however difficult that may be. And we resist lust because promiscuity obviously strengthens the lower self—even though desire itself, if sublimated and beautified by love, can become a power to take us closer to the Divine. So through our struggles we gradually succeed. But a more difficult temptation is the desire to excel in occult techniques. Many yogis who face this do not succeed in overcoming it, but succumb to the temptations of omnipotent powers that others, such as Christ and Buddha, have also been tempted with. We read that many of them have been offered this power, as symbolized by Christ's temptation at the beginning of the New Testament where Satan—that is, the Satan-principle—asks him to exercise these powers over the world and become its ruler. Significantly, just before Christ emerges in his ministry the temptation that he faces isn't greed, anger, or lust, but the temptation to control the world by means of his mystic and occult powers. Christ didn't succumb. But he too had to face this last temptation.

But the real argument against the occult, in the sense of seeking and using powers to benefit ourselves, is that, more than any other activity, it feeds the ego directly. The proof is that after we have removed all the other difficulties, all the other deadly sins, the desire for occult power remains. And according to the authoritative *Yoga Aphorisms* of Patanjali, the desire to exercise control over others is the most difficult temptation to withstand. This temptation comes to the spiritual seeker in the form of psychic powers and the occult. All of this lies within the mind, and at a certain point these powers become available to us. We have to bypass the temptation in order to go farther into the mind and continue our spiritual progress. The realm of the psychic and the realm of the psychotic both lie within us. We need to negotiate all of these different channels or levels of consciousness: psychotic, psychic, mystical.

Many people have psychotic experiences in which they seem to act like mystics. They become withdrawn, trance-like, and enter

The Psychic and the Psychotic

into a domain of their own, so that, loosely speaking, we could use the word *mystical* about them—albeit inaccurately. The difference between the psychotic and the mystical experience is that in the first you emerge deranged, and in the latter you emerge transformed. They have only outward similarities; they are radically different in their results and consequences.

In the world of the subconscious, the world that we study in depth during our meditation, we discover the covert patterns of the ego-mind. One of the possibilities of this is the neurotic or the psychotic option. We see the way these negative tendencies form in the mind, and we have to overcome them: We must be strong and not yield to them. There is a temptation to yield to neurosis and to the various kinds of mental illness that we are all prone to. We shouldn't be shocked when these mental states emerge in us; we need to be aware of them. Ignorance of these states is a liability we all face: Those who are weak or uninformed may succumb to them. As we advance on the spiritual path there are times when we feel like giving in to negative moods that can lead only to some kind of neurosis, anxiety, or depression—those floating dragons in the sea of the subconscious that we learn to circumvent through spiritual practices and self-knowledge.

Also within us is the world of the psychic. Some people— often those who have advanced a considerable way in the spiritual life—deliberately and systematically seek psychic powers for their own aggrandizement. These powers are an extension of ego-devices in an unfamiliar realm, a reappearance of the desires and cravings of the ego. The familiar patterns of egoism in the world of the senses are carried on into the psychic, invisible realm. The same motivations, the same problems are there.

After we have overcome all of these formidable obstacles and temptations, we gain great power as a result. You mean it is offered

Emptiness - The Void to us as a kind of reward for giving up greed and lust? No. Greed and lust, anger and hatred are veils that cover up the light of ourselves. Gradually, as we remove these veils, the light comes through more and more. Nothing is given to us, because everything is already present. The coverings are just removed, one by one—hence the emphasis on Emptiness, which some are puzzled by, or the Void. Both seem negative, but they are not. Emptiness is Brahman, because It is empty of everything that is not true, that is not essential, that is not divine—that is Brahman of the Hindus, and the Emptiness of Buddhism. The Void is that which remains when we remove everything that is nonessential. The Void, the word used to represent this reality, is not negative at all. It is positive. That also is Brahman—the Absolute, the Self.

In meditation we concentrate on some idea of our own choosing that symbolizes the Reality within. We cling to that symbol so that the mind has some comfortable way to advance into the unknown country within itself. In the process of meditation we empty ourselves of the things that are distracting us. We gently turn our mind away from the world. But when we do this, we discover it isn't a true emptiness, because after we have emptied the contents of the outer world we discover the seething world within—and it is not so empty after all! But we are to do the same thing there as we proceed. In principle, we start out the same way. We sit for meditation and we detach our mind from the false, the accidental, the habitual, the nonessential. Detachment is just another word for emptying the mind. There is a sense of peace when we do that, as though there is already a glimpse of what true peace really might be, the peace that passeth understanding, even on the outer limits of the mind. As we reach ever-deeper levels, we continually detach ourselves from nonessentials. To start with, we empty the mind from all the clutter of the day, such as whom we saw yesterday, or whether we are going to get that job, or whether we'll buy that book or not. There is a little peace right away. And we empty the mind, too, of all the other things that are nonessential, little by little, slowly, in a controlled way. Lust, greed, anger, hatred, jealousy, envy all fall away. These sins are deadly because they conceal the light from us. We are full of light; we *are* light. The soul's nature *is* light, not merely the light that we see, but another light—the Light of the Self.

If we can empty ourselves of the things that conceal the Light, we go into the emptiness—into God, into Brahman, into the Void. The Void, then, is the realization of the essential. It is that which results when the nonessential is voided, is removed, is emptied. Those sins are deadly because they provide not merely a few, but hundreds of veils concealing the Light of the Self. We have to give them up. But even then we are not purged of the ego itself, which has been responsible for all of them and is the central enemy that has to be fought down.

After we have removed the other appendages, these false additions that we think are so necessary to our existence ("Sometimes you have to be angry, and you have to be somewhat greedy, otherwise you can't support yourself"), what remains is the villain that has produced them: this ego-consciousness that says, "I." And after removing all the ego's lifelines, its feeder-lines, it still remains like a spider without its web. We've driven it into a corner, but the spider remains when its web has been destroyed, the web of all this false life. But although we've emptied it of its web, we still haven't reached the end.

The ego remains. It stands on this triumph and says, "I have done all this. Show me one other person who has done all this; show me one other person in this whole nation who has done all this." Pride is also a phase of ego in one of its obvious forms. Even a yogi may experience this involuntary rush of ego-consciousness, which comes when we have done any great thing. How do we become free of this ego? It is a long, long struggle.

For example, you reach a point where you do some good deed and find yourself regretting that no one noticed what you did. You feel unappreciated. One

Devotional vs. Non-Devotional Approaches

solution is to discriminate about this, asking yourself: "Why did I do this? Did I do it to get attention?" You begin to criticize yourself and detach yourself from the part of you that wants to be noticed, the ego. That's the path of discrimination, the Buddhist or the Zen approach, loosely speaking. We can always use it to some extent. The other approach is to pray to the Deity, or to your idea of God, for help: "Free me from this obsession. Please free me from this delusion, this ego." And somehow or other, help comes.

Ideally we should incorporate and make use of the different yogas depending on the mood and situation. We go from one approach to the other. On the one hand, if we are in a prayerful mood, we should exercise devotion. We shouldn't think, "I'm not on the devotional path; I'm following the approach of Zen." We might be passing up a priceless opportunity. On the other hand, if we are on the devotional path and a mood of very austere discrimination comes in which we are very self-reproachful, self-analytical, we shouldn't think: "I mustn't do that because I'm on the path of devotion." We should certainly take advantage of *that*. Both approaches are necessary; both will help us against the ego's last stronghold.

How might prayer be answered at such a time? If prayer is answered, we are freed from the desire for a reward. The thing that is scourging us, that is blocking us, is the desire to be rewarded, to be noticed. This obstacle on the spiritual path is the ego. We can try various ways to get around it. One way to get around it is to pray to be released. So if the prayer is answered, then paradoxically we will be released from the desire for the reward itself. It seems natural to seek a reward, but any action we undertake should be for its own sake. We should take the karma yoga approach and act just for the sake of action, for the sake of the good in the action, and not to be rewarded personally. We benefit spiritually if we don't seek a reward from other sources. As Henry David Thoreau wrote, "Rescue the drowning and tie your shoestrings." Then we benefit by the reward that comes of its own in the sense of peace, of selflessness, which is a nonegoistic reward. The reward that the ego seeks—attention, recognition, applause—is something else again. What we really want is to be freed from the desire to seek recognition. If we could be freed from that egoistic attachment, we would be happy. If prayer can help us achieve this goal and thereby overcome desire, then we should make use of it.

Consider Buddha's teaching: Desire, craving, is the cause of all unhappiness and sorrow. The embodied self seeks to continue to exist at any cost, and the desires that accompany this state—such as cravings, attachments, and aversions—are false desires. He compared this whole network of phenomena to fire. The mind is on fire, the senses are on fire; all burn with the fire of craving, the cause of sorrow. Buddha's objective was to put out the fire.

The desire for liberation, however, is not considered a desire in this context—and yet it is indeed a desire. Imagine waves of the ocean coming onto the shore one after the other; each swell disturbing the serenity of the ocean is like a wave of desire. Then a huge wave comes and swallows them all up—this huge wave is the desire for liberation, or for the love of God, or for self-realization. So we see desire swallowing up desire.

But don't we need the ego self in order to get along in the world? There may be some confusion here between the ego self and the self we feel we have to become in order to get along in the world. Are they the same or not? They are not the same. We may be concerned that in pursuing the natural development of our ordinary individual self in its nonharmful dimension that somehow we are developing the harmful egoistic self.

When we use the word *ego* it is meant strictly in the sense of this undermining, self-destructive entity, the perverse shadow self that is the adversary in Christ's terminology, or the Spectre in William Blake's. The ego is behind desire, anger, lust, hatred, jealousy, and envy.

At the other extreme there is the Soul, the supreme Self, the still-unrealized Atman that starts to emerge, beckoning us on. We feel its grace, its illumination, and its presence.

We can think of the individual self as having two parts. One, its harmful aspect, is the one we mean when we usually refer to the ego, and the other is its nonharmful aspect, the ordinary individual self in us, which is basically good. When this benign part becomes diseased—self-loving, self-serving to the exclusion of others—we call it egoism, egotism, or egocentricity. That is really what we are referring to when we say ego.

But to develop our spiritual life, particularly as active people, we need to have a strong character, a healthy personality. We have to build up our personalities to become strong, but not in the sense of ego-strong, or the sense of self-will. It is most important that the foundation of our personalities must be sound for spiritual realization to come. For instance, we must have self-reliance and self-confidence. We have to build these up in ways that come to us naturally through jobs, relationships, interests, activities, decisions, acceptances, renunciations. We have to be strong in order to do the day's work well, to relate to others, and to carry our share of the burden of life. We have to have self-respect and self-esteem; if we don't, the mind tends to become depressed easily, and sinks into needless states of anxiety with feelings like "I'm not capable, I can't do this, I'm not as good as they are," and so on. Hence, we need to strengthen this individual part of ourselves so that it will not yield to the temptations of the ego, but yield to the temptation of the great Self that is calling us onward.

This aspect of the mind-stuff[*] that we need to strengthen is

---

[*] The Sanskrit term for the mind-stuff or inner organ is *Antahkarana:* It is analyzed in the Sankhya philosophy as *Manas,* the mind or receptive faculty that operates out of desire; *Buddhi,* the intellect or determinative faculty; *Chitta,* the memory storehouse; and *Ahamkara,* the sense of ego.

called the *buddhi* or intellect. It is the faculty of discernment, which opposes the ego. The buddhi is the mind in its decisive mode, which helps us to make the right decisions.

At every moment our ordinary self identifies with either the buddhi or the ego. The former is aligned with the Universal Soul, the Divine, the Godhead within, and the latter with the adversary, the Spectre, the Satan within. Christ and Satan: These are the contraries, the polarities. And *you,* the individual self that stands between them, is the one who says, "I will meditate," or "I won't meditate." It decides every moment of every day whether we will identify with the ego or with Brahman. To the degree that it identifies with the former it becomes egocentric; to the degree that it identifies with the latter it becomes spiritual and eventually holy.

We are like people who live far inland and have heard about the ocean, a body of salt water that is said to spread for thousands of miles. Someone who has come from the ocean (the ocean of Brahman) tells us that It is real: If you can see It, touch It, you become immortal. This sounds unbelievable, but we want to see for ourselves, so we gradually make our way towards It. Even though we are now thousands of miles away from that ocean, in the midst of the prairie, we begin our journey anyway. We believe in the scripture, or in our teacher, or in the description of this ocean, and we go forward. For a long time there are no signs of progress—but still we strive.

Meanwhile, as we travel towards the ocean we get stronger, **The Ego and the** little by little. Perhaps ten or twenty miles from **Occult** our destination we begin to enter a different atmosphere. The country changes, the fields become greener; we encounter another kind of landscape. Still we haven't seen the shore. But increasingly we find ourselves with different companions—holy people who say, "You're getting closer, keep going." And as we proceed, we've lost our anger, greed, craving— and the loss of these things has brought us closer to the shore and made our minds stronger and more pure. And as we unburden ourselves and finally reach an advanced point, we say, "How far I've come, what a great distance I've come. I thank God that I am not like other men." So the ego, purged of its grossest sins, takes credit for these accomplishments. Also with these accomplishments come occult powers that emerge as part of the advance towards the ocean of Brahman. Now comes the temptation to exercise occult or psychic powers, to dominate other people's minds, to appear to be a mysterious sage.

If we yield to the ego's desire to dominate others, we stop growing and gradually we fall back to a lower state. And when we're thwarted, anger returns. Lust comes into play, too—all the vices come back. These things are not killed off until we reach the ocean and merge into It. Even if we've gone all the way to the shore, these forces are merely held in check. The difference between the near-yogi and the ignorant man is that the near-yogi has everything under control. The ignorant man is controlled by his subconscious, by his drives. The near-yogi or the near-saint has everything under control, but the negative potential still exists. It is only when the advanced soul enters into the ocean of Brahman that all of these potentialities are wiped out.

So this last temptation directly serves the ego at its final outpost. At any step of the way, however, this enticement faces us. Even if we've just begun to meditate, the thought may occur:

"Now perhaps I can control people and read their minds." Near the end of the spiritual journey, when there's nothing else remaining, this is the ego's last feeder-line.

Patanjali, the ancient Indian authority on yoga powers, explains what these occult powers are and then warns against them. The purpose of yoga, of spiritual disciplines, is to go beyond all occult powers in order to reach the ocean of Brahman, to experience Self-realization. We must overcome this temptation to assert ourselves on the occult plane.

Emerson's poem "Brahma" concludes:

> But thou, meek lover of the good!
> Find me, and turn thy back on heaven.

When we become a meek lover of the good, and humbly desire only the good, then we are able to turn our back on these occult powers, which divert us from the true goal—which is not heaven, but the ocean of Brahman.

By now we have smelled the salt breeze in the air. The closer we get to the ocean, the more the atmosphere changes. If we can overcome these last temptations, then we will finally see the ocean of Brahman. Perhaps we will even enter It and become that Ocean.

Let us now turn our attention to some of the great spiritual masters from other mystic traditions and teachings to see how these truths of Vedanta are corroborated in their experiences of that Ocean.

PART FOUR

Truth Is One:
Sages Call It by
Different Names

One of the glories of mysticism is its universality. Perhaps its two chief treasures are its power to transform life as nothing else can, and its perennial appearance in religion after religion through millennia after millennia.

Vedanta claims to be this universal mysticism, its principles the principles underlying every religion, its truth the eternal truth of every faith.

Let us see how this in fact is the case by touching upon the teachings of certain outstanding individual mystics who seem at first sight to stand apart from the tradition we've looked at so far.

13

 # Plotinus

Plotinus was a dominant voice in the Platonic mystique, coming about four or five centuries after Plato himself and active in both Alexandria and Rome. By then—approximately 200 A.D.—the mystical tradition of Neo-Platonism was at its peak in the underground world of mysticism in the Near East, Egypt, and Rome. Neo-Platonism had borrowed something from Christianity, but Christianity as a whole was still underground, while Neo-Platonism remained respectable: Plotinus, for example, was an honored teacher in his own time. In addition, Neo-Platonism was indebted to the influence of India, which has always constituted a kind of atmospheric vibration all through the centuries for spiritual seekers.[67]

Plotinus writes that a man has failed in life "if he fails to win this and only this"[68]—the mystical experience. This experience **The Mystical** should be open to all of us, even though we are **Experience** at different stages. Anyone who has eyes to see and a mind to think with should have access to it. Plotinus makes a strong statement here, implying that a person who hasn't gained an awareness of the Divine within himself or herself and in the world hasn't begun to live. No matter what else we have discovered, we occupy at best a twilight zone, winning trophies and fame perhaps but never coming to know the Light. We live like the people in Plato's cave—excelling in a life of shadows but never realizing the light that might illumine their path.

Plotinus says, "Shut your eyes and ... apprehend [the Truth] by spiritual intuition." This capacity increases until it becomes the thing it is apprehending. Where does the light of truth come from? "This light comes from the One and is the One."[69] It is almost as though Plotinus has read the Upanishads, but it is almost certain he hadn't. Plotinus, and Eckhart later on, seem familiar with the Indian scriptures—but it was not their learning that gave them the same consciousness and the same insights; it was their superconscious experiences.

"How then can this come to us? Strip thyself of everything."[70] Here Plotinus presents the monastic idea. Though Plotinus mingled with men as an esteemed teacher, he was essentially a monastic, as was Eckhart. We need not follow their example; we shouldn't have to renounce physically so much as mentally, and then not all at once. We live in a different world from Plotinus and Eckhart. Although we don't deny the truth of their teachings, the way set forth to realize them has to be modified. We are not the same people now, and civilization has made so many other things available that the older, simpler way of willed renunciation is not the only alternative—though some will still want to take this path.

Nevertheless, we must gradually strip away the nonessentials from our lives—recalling the idea of Emptiness presented earlier, the removal of all nonessentials. This is for certain. We don't have to leave our home or our job, but we have to strip the mind of the things that encumber our meditation, and this is where spiritual exercises guide us. That is, when our meditation is obstructed we find more often than not that it's because we are clinging to some activity, image, thought, or attitude that is expendable. When we drop it, there is a lightening and clarification of the mind that makes meditation more integrated.

What is this One, this union with the One? It is, according to Plotinus, that union of which the merging of lovers is an imitation.

Divine Union In brief, the union of lovers is the attempt to unite with the One, the attempt to destroy the separateness of egoism in the experience of a divine and larger unity—a view of the love relationship according to a realized soul.

The mystic sees everything in the world as symbolic, as William Blake, among others, has told us. Everything is an emblem of something else—even though to us, immersed in this world, it is not symbolic but real. If we think of two lovers being together, we dwell on the realistic aspects, whereas, the mystic cannot help but see their embrace metaphorically.

Take dreams, for example. Some are just distorted recountings of the day's events, without pattern or significance. But in important dreams everything is symbolic; these dreams tell a story in pictures, without the necessity for words. They allegorize a truth that we don't know yet, but which the subconscious mind knows. It tries to send a message up to consciousness through the means of stories. As we remember a dream, it is clearly symbolic, not realistic at all. The mystic sees the world in the same light. Even though living in the world with other people, the mystic responds to it as though it was a dream.

When in this state the soul would exchange its present

condition for nothing, no, not for the [highest] heaven of heavens. For there is nothing more blessed than this.[71]

Here Plotinus describes the experience of the One. Heaven, as we may remember from Emerson's poem "Brahma," is a

Heaven

limited place: "But thou, meek lover of the good, find me and turn thy back on heaven." In this view—the view of the Upanishads and of Taoism, as we'll see shortly—heaven, though real enough, is merely a state of enjoyment that will come to an end sooner or later, since it is the result of desire and good intentions aimed at gaining heaven and its rewards.

Anything produced in this manner must come to an end; the good karma, as the Hindus or Buddhists would call it, will eventually wear out. Any kind of desire, good or bad, will produce its consequences in this world or some other. If we perform sacrifices, rituals, or prayers with the idea of getting rewards from them, we may well be rewarded, but with time the reward will be exhausted. Heaven is not infinite nor eternal since the actions that produced it were not; the attitudes behind it were limited coming from the finite mind. As we advance on the spiritual path this idea of enjoying heaven becomes less of an ideal to be cherished and more and more a distraction.

Heaven is not a place for further advancement, rather a realm where one can rest on laurels achieved on earth. Heaven won't bring us closer to Truth: We would be so diverted by celestial pleasures that we would forget the main business of the search for universal truth. "Find me and turn thy back on heaven," writes Emerson. But it's not that heaven doesn't exist. We have heard there are many heavens. But again, these heavens would simply provide the same pleasures and delights available here, only on a more exquisite scale. All this is irrelevant to someone who has glimpsed something higher. Plotinus continues:

> [The happiness of the soul] is no titillation of the bodily senses; it is that the soul has become again what it was formerly, when it was blessed. All the things which once pleased it, power, wealth, beauty, science, it declares that it despises.[72]

We were once blest, long ago—not in childhood, but in some earlier existence of which we get intimations from time to time in unexpected ways, luring us on to deepen our search. The experience of *déjà vu* is one of the plausible evidences of reincarnation, when suddenly a strange town, event, or person is entirely familiar to us. But here the idea is presented on a much grander scale. It is the experience of "coming home": "It is that the soul has become again what it was formerly, when it was blessed."

"All the things which once pleased it … it declares that it *despises*"—that's a strong word. Will we despise all these worldly offerings? Not knowledge, certainly. But the mystic declares that in relation to this experience even the boon of knowledge is an insipid and shadowy thing, quickly forgotten.

> The vision is confounded with the object seen, and that which was before [the] object becomes to him the state of seeing, and he forgets all else.[73]

What is the vision of the One Life? "The vision is confounded

The Vision of Truth with the object seen." Thus we have the individual seeker and also the object being sought, either in the sense of a spiritual reality or of some divine form that we may choose to dwell on. There is the individual and then *That.* The two seem separate, but so many of the mystics have emphasized the oneness of the experience. In some mysterious way, the searcher and the object of the search become one; you become that which you are looking for. So we have the act of seeing, the vision, and the object of the vision: "That which was the object becomes to him the state of seeing," or that which was previously the object of his search, of his meditation and his vision, in fact becomes the power by which he sees and the state of seeing itself—"and he forgets all else."

And the chief obstacle to the vision?

As ... one cannot think of two things at once ... so here ... it is impossible for one who has in his soul any extraneous image to conceive of the One.[74]

Again, we have the idea of stripping away. As we'll see in the next section, according to Lao Tzu the world is won—little by little—by those who let it go. Gradually, distracting things have to be dropped; the veils that hide the One have to be cast aside, and then the One emerges.

"Men flee away from him, or rather from themselves." There is no real difference between the One and the Many—"But he who has learned to know himself will know from whence he is." And what is that center within us, that source? "We touch the center of all things with our own center."[75]

Plotinus speaks in the quiet language of the mystics; he has no desire to overpower with illustrations or rhetoric. He feels that those who know what he is talking about won't need much emphasis anyway, and those who don't know won't understand the truth of his message any more than the spoon can understand the taste of the soup. Just as the tongue can taste the soup, a person partially enlightened can taste the truth of the mystics. But a person who has not reached that point is like a spoon in soup. This is Buddha's image for the vast differences in human potentiality for spiritual life.

Plotinus uses the symbol of the dance to evoke the harmony between the soul and what it has experienced: "In this choral dance the soul sees the fountain of life and the fountain of Spirit."[76] The person who has experienced Truth becomes all-powerful: Such a person inherits the earth and can do whatever he or she wishes. But more often than not he or she is content with simply *being*. Some saints and yogis have exercised that power, for good no doubt, and fabulous things are reported about them. Plotinus hints at this. In other words, if a person enters into Nirvana or achieves self-realization, everything in the universe is open to him or her. As we heard in the *Chandogya Upanishad,* the realized soul is *That.*

In this experience "we see ourselves as pure, subtle, ethereal, light; we become divine, or rather we know ourselves to be divine."[77] It isn't that at some point in time we are mortal and then after a certain experience we become divine. Rather, we discover that all along we were divine; we were Light all the time, and not darkness.

> But in the vision, that which sees is not reason, but something greater than and prior to reason…. In this state the seer … ceases to be himself and to belong to himself.[78]

Reason is asleep; the senses are asleep; the body is still. At that time the seeker "ceases to be himself"—that is, the old self, the old sense of individuality. Such a person just ceases to belong to himself, like one who has discarded a coat and then forgets about it.

> This is no doubt why in the mysteries we are forbidden
> to reveal them to the uninitiated.[79]

Here Plotinus refers to the experience as being ineffable; it therefore cannot be expressed to the uninitiated. But this also

The Old Monastic Ideal

reflects the monastic ideal that secrets should not be revealed to novices. But it is too late for that now. Despite the risks involved in having these ideas misconstrued, misunderstood, and used for selfish motives by those who are not yet ready for them, we have to reveal everything to the world and we have to discover everything. It is still a sensible idea not to cast your best insights or pearls before the unappreciative—as Jesus warned in the Sermon on the Mount—for they may turn on you. At the same time these secrets can no longer be confined to the few in monasteries and hermitages. We have such a hunger for Truth now that everything is being revealed to us.

Plotinus' viewpoint was the monastic ideal for thousands of years. In the space of just the last century or so the practice of keeping this esoteric knowledge secret has changed. We have in America gurus, swamis, lamas, and yogis from the Orient. Many of them are legitimate teachers, highly advanced souls, who have come to the West to share their knowledge and wisdom. Not so long ago, this would have been unheard of—these teachers would have said that they can't reveal such things to the uninitiated. This shift intimates that the world has reached such a pass that we can't afford the luxury of a spiritual caste system.

> He knows that it is by the first Principle that we see the
> first Principle.[80]

It is by God that we see God, by the Divine that we see the Divine, by the grace of the Self that we see the Self. This state of mystical union is poetically described by Plotinus as "A flight of the alone to the Alone."[81]

14

 Lao Tzu

Let us turn to Lao Tzu's *Tao Te Ching* or *The Way of Life* and focus on one of his aphorisms (presented in verse form) on the idea of "stripping thyself of everything":

> The student learns by daily increment.
> The Way is gained by daily loss,
> Loss upon loss until
> At last comes rest.
>
> By letting go, it all gets done;
> The world is won by those who let it go!
> But when you try and try,
> The world is then beyond the winning.[82]

Lao Tzu was the founder of Taoism. *The Way* is his term for Brahman, for God. By this he isn't referring to a different reality,

The Way

but simply a different approach to it. The Way evokes the same encounter but in the Chinese manner. Often it is a cultural emphasis rather than the viewpoint of an individual mystic that brings about the different terms they use. Some peoples have more of a craving for subtleties than others, and the Chinese are well known for this.

"The student learns by daily increment," via discursive reasoning. As Plotinus said, by nature we take things separately, adding this, subtracting that—in Lao Tzu's language, "daily increment." The Way, however, "is gained by daily loss." The Way suggests an impersonal reality moving upon and influencing everything.

The Way is gained by daily loss ... until at last comes rest.

Rest is the discovery of the Self. The Way in fact is the Self. It can't be separate from us. At first it seems that if we don't obey the Way—or don't obey the Lord, or Brahman, or the Truth—we'll suffer. In that sense we seem separate from the power coercing us into line, urging us, instructing us, to be moral and spiritual. The Truth, or the Law, or God, or the Way is one thing, and we are another. It does seem as though we are separate.

But as we've seen, it is the ego-self that feels separate and gets itself into trouble. As we learn more of the nature of the Way, we get closer to It and feel less and less that It is separate from us. Gradually we feel united. And that which was suffering, that which felt separate from the Way, is no more—it is simply the darkness that disappears with the light of the Way.

With the help of meditation and other spiritual exercises we deal with the problem of separateness; we enthrone the higher self deliberately by an act of will, and impose it on the lower self. We try to do this at least for a few times every day so that the feeling of separateness from that which is instructing us—sometimes painfully—decreases, resulting in moments during our spiritual practice when we feel at one with something much greater than ourselves. Then the thought occurs that perhaps we *are* that, and the Way then doesn't feel at all apart from us—we seem to *be* the Way.

"The Way is gained by daily loss"—meaning gradual loss, little by little. Socrates walked the streets of Athens, looked in all the shop windows, and remarked how many things there were in the world that he did not want. After a while, we see many things that we don't want either. Right now, however, we think we need them. But as we drop the expendables, we slowly come to identify with the Way.

Letting Go of Nonessentials

"Loss upon loss"—loss of the nonessential—"until at last comes rest." This is not dullness, not the rest of the grave, but the rest of an eagle dallying with the wind, controlling itself while in repose. This is the repose of the sun in the meridian. It is the rest of complete equipoise in which all the elements, within and without, are in a state of relaxed control.

This condition is beyond willpower. Will is necessary to reach it—to renounce the nonessentials, to strip the mind to its essence, to meditate. This struggle takes willpower, and will is essential for self-realization. But the state of rest that Lao Tzu describes here is beyond the will. When we have come into that rest—our Self, our own being—the will has served its purpose and we have no more need of it.

"By letting go, it all gets done." This refers to letting go of the ego-self that habitually feels, "If I don't manage things they will not get done... unless I am in the midst of things they will fall apart." But in fact the Way is what gets things done. Restraining the senses and the ordinary mind, we let the Way work through us.

The world is won by those who let it go!

The world that is won, however, is not the realm of the senses, but the world of the Infinite. Everything you ever wanted *deeply* is won by letting it all go. To achieve the goal, we need to stop clinging to things; we need to become detached, and strip away what is unnecessary. This is one more paradox for us to absorb. Spiritual life is full of them.

> But when you try and try,
> The world is then beyond the winning.

Impelled by rajas, the ego tries and tries to win the world. But Lao Tzu tells us that if we try and try the "world is then beyond the winning." It seems as though he is telling us to do nothing, to give in to tamas, when he says, "the world is won by those who let it go." And yet we shouldn't try and try either. So what is really being recommended is a middle path between inertia and blind self-assertion, in short, between the gunas of tamas and rajas.

The challenge is subtle: How does one find the poise of sattva between the two extremes of tamas and rajas? Balance plays a **Practical Renunciation** vital role in spiritual life—it is not easy to accomplish, but one can learn how to achieve it. This balance requires a kind of enlightened nonattachment, such as we see in a nurse or a police officer. We should continue to do everything we are doing—at home or on the job, anywhere—but perform our duties in a spirit of detachment. That is the renunciation called for—not a letting go of job or responsibilities. It is a renunciation of the clinging ego that says, "I must do this. I must have this." We should be motivated by enlightened nonattachment and renounce the ego.

Notice, for example, the way in which a nurse is nonattached, but at the same time sympathetic to his or her patients. When *we* come to the hospital to see the person we are there to visit, we are attached. From the point of view of actual helpfulness, we don't do any more good to the invalid than the nurse does. He or she can be even more helpful, and can be sympathetic to many patients, yet in a detached manner. Another example is the police officer who does his or her job without feeling that he or she is the one doing it—rather it is the law working through him or her that is the source of authority. That outlook is our objective too.

> The Way is gained by daily loss,
> Loss upon loss until at last comes rest.
>
> By letting go, it all gets done ...

Another interpretation of the phrase "loss upon loss" is meekness. As Christ says: "Blessed are the meek, for they shall

Meekness

inherit the earth." (Matthew 5: 5) The world is won by the meek, for they shall know the Way. They shall inherit the Divine Power that rules the world, because they will be united with that Divinity. There will be nothing in them any longer to prevent It from filling them, and then they become That.

The meek person, then, is meek towards the Way, towards God, towards the Truth—meek in the sense of humble or selfless, not in the sense of crestfallen. *Meek* is a pejorative term in English. It is not the best word we could use in that famous line from the Beatitudes. It seems almost unattractive. But here the term *meek* simply means to be humble towards the Infinite, towards Truth. The meek, therefore, inherit the earth—not in the sense of gaining worldly power but in the context of divine consciousness, of being the chosen instrument of the Way, which is always seeking to find someone It can work through. Finally when it does, It gives that individual everything. However, this doesn't apply to the person who still feels that he or she is the doer:

> But when you try and try,
> The world is then beyond the winning.

15

 Meister Eckhart

We turn to another great seer, Meister Eckhart, whose thunder-bolts of insight based on his mystical experience, we have not forgotten. Living in Germany about 1300, Eckhart was perhaps the chief Christian mystic. He was a monk, but so independent of traditional Christian teaching that he could have been a layman. After his death the Catholic authorities firmly ex-communicated him because of his outlaw beliefs.

Among his heresies was the declaration that the Trinity is merely a way by which the Godhead structures itself for the sake of human intellect. According to Eckhart, the Father, the Son and the Holy Ghost are channels to realization of supernal truth, but not the Truth itself. Beyond the Son, beyond the Holy Ghost, beyond the Father, there is That of which these are emanations— so declared this Catholic monk in the fourteenth century.

> God and the Soul are so nearly [related] to each other
> that there is really no distinction between them.[83]

Over and over Eckhart stresses that the unity of the Soul is indistinguishable from the unity of the Godhead. From this unity arises the vast multiplicity of all the things that seem real to us:

Unity of the Soul and the Godhead

our sensations, our thoughts, and our awareness of our sensations and thoughts. These are elements we exclude from our meditation more and more as we come to realize that they lie on the periphery of our minds, that they are not consciousness any more than the objects in a lighted room are the light in that room. A room in darkness reveals nothing but darkness. If you turn on the light, you see not the light but everything else. Remove the objects, the light remains; remove the light, the darkness returns. The light is the reality, not the things that the light reveals.

We mistakenly believe that the contents of our consciousness, like the objects in a room, represent consciousness itself. Rather our consciousness is like the light, and the furniture of our minds is composed of our images, thoughts, sensations, even our philosophies—these are like the objects in the room, its furniture interchangeable with other objects that could be put there.

In meditation we gradually detach the consciousness from the things that clutter up the mind and make us think that that is what we are, and what the mind is. Little by little, we continue to detach ourselves from all of that until ideally what remains is consciousness itself, the light *behind,* after which the mind may function as a reflector of that light.

The mind is not consciousness; the mind is the perceiving instrument by which consciousness is experienced. The mind is the magnifying lens that starts the fire; consciousness is the sun. But the mind cannot perceive properly unless these objects—images, ideas, volitions—are gradually seen for the obstructions that they are, and discarded. These objects are expendable miscellanies of experience that have no abiding reality and no special significance. We simply have to detach ourselves from all of them.

If we can achieve that detachment, then when we return to ordinary consciousness from meditation and we encounter them

Freedom from Attachment

again in our home, at work, in our social life—those faces, images, sensations which in our spiritual practice we have been learning to regard as merely the phenomena of the mind and not essentially the mind—we no longer relate to them with the same clinging attachment. There is serenity now, a feeling of balance. If they depart, we don't feel bereft. If they suddenly insult us, or take something from us, we don't feel that we have to react. Our meditation has taught us that these things are not our reality, but something else is. The mind, because of spiritual discipline, has been conditioned to regard them now in a different mode, and the attachment is no longer there, or not so automatic. There is a feeling of becoming free. In other areas of the mind we are still bound, still enthralled to the past, and we work on those resistances until over time we attain still greater freedom.

Gradually we turn more and more to the sun, to the inner light. The process goes on for months and years. As we return to the world, we learn to approach our problems in a more kindly, compassionate, and impersonal way. We are not harsh or austere: Being impersonal or detached does not mean we are inhumane. On the contrary, as we noted, many people—nurses, doctors, teachers—are impersonal and yet friendly and sympathetic.

Buddha was known for his detachment. Making no distinctions, he treated everyone and everything in the same way—and yet he was the epitome of compassion. So we must not allow the mind to think that detachment means coldness and inhumanity. Rather, it is a dynamic new way of approaching the things that typically clutch at us, seize us, and make us act against our better judgment. We have to respond in a more enlightened manner. If this means being more impersonal than we have been, we should cultivate that attitude.

> The eye by which I see God is the same as the eye by which God sees me. My eye and God's eye are one and the same.[84]

This is a powerful and dramatic statement. It is exciting to find the same theme of the oneness of the individual Soul and the Divine Being persisting in unlikely places: Plotinus in Rome and Alexandria of the third century A.D., Eckhart in the Rhine Valley during the fourteenth century, the Upanishadic sages on the banks of the Ganges before 1000 B.C.

> By nature the core of the soul is sensitive to nothing but the divine Being, unmediated. Here God enters the soul with all he has and not in part.[85]

This immense declaration is set down quietly, as though Eckhart, having experienced what he writes of, doesn't feel he needs to prove anything.

He speaks of the new birth, the awakening of the spiritual consciousness out of its material bondage:

> Do not imagine that your own intelligence may arise to it.... The natural light must in fact be completely extinguished before God will shine in with his light, bringing back with him all that you have forsaken....[86]

Christ says, "Seek ye first the kingdom of God and his righteousness and all other things will be added unto you." (Matthew 6: 33) If we seek the Divine within and we find it, then everything else will come—if, as Ramakrishna remarked, you really want it. Once you have had the experience of the Divine, you may not want the other things you have abandoned en route in order to realize Him. But if we want them we can have them:

Seeking the Divine

> God will shine in with his light, bringing back with him
> all that you have forsaken and a thousand times more,
> together with a new form to contain it all.

By "new form" Eckhart here refers to a new inner body. In addition to the physical entity we all see, there is also an astral or spiritual body that interpenetrates the physical form. The inner, the spiritual body contains spiritual blessings, not the outer, physical one. In addition to this new spiritual body, a changed nervous system and brain structure would be provided for this transformed consciousness. To paraphrase Ramakrishna, after ecstasy every pore in the body becomes a sexual organ, so that the experience of divine joy is inconceivably greater than the most intense human pleasure.

> There is no rest for the mind until it has attained all that
> is possible to it.... Do not imagine that God is like a
> carpenter who works or not, just as he pleases.... It is not
> so with God, for when he finds you ready he must act,
> and pour into you....[87]

Once we have awakened to the possibility of spiritual enlightenment, there can be no turning back. We are free to do so, but what would we gain? Even if it involves suffering and struggle, we have to press on.

"When the channel of purity is open," wrote Thoreau, "the soul immediately flies to God."[88] Ramakrishna declared that the devotee has God under his control and God must respond to his bidding. Eckhart says essentially the same thing. If you are ready, God must act: He has no choice in the matter. Not that He would want to have a choice—would the sun want to deny its light? The sun *must* give out its light: The moment the way is clear, it must pour through.

"The soul ranks so high that it communes with God ... as he is."[89] These lofty teachings are an effective antidote to the idea of

The Soul's Communion with God

God upon which most of us in the West were raised—that God is something far away from us, possibly in heaven, and we are here, quite apart, reaching Him occasionally through prayer.

This notion lingers in the recesses of consciousness. It is like saying, "I know the energy in the universe exists, but I myself feel somewhat separate from it." In fact, we are one with that energy as much as any other particle of life is, the energy being omnipresent, indivisible. The energy is in all of us: we can't be apart from it because it is coursing through us at all times. So it is with the God we heard was far away in heaven. What we were told simply isn't true, and we have to shake off the delusion completely in order to proceed towards our liberation.

Unless we are very saintly to begin with, it is hard to proceed on the basis of this ignorant conception of the Deity. If you are a saintly person and believe that we are separate from God, sooner or later you will have a divine experience and you will know the truth. It behooves the rest of us who are struggling towards saintliness to shake off that old conception and remember that "The soul ranks so high that it communes with God ... as he is."

"In eternity," says Eckhart, "the Father begets the Son in his own likeness." Or, we might say that God begets the soul in His own likeness. By *eternity* Eckhart is referring to the mystical experience. Eternity is not somewhere out in space or time. It is where you are, here and now. The mystical experience is eternity apprehended. "[God] begets me not only as his Son but as Himself ... in his own nature.... and with no distinction between us."[90] In Eckhart's time the Church authorities wouldn't accept this. But we do. Even though we haven't had his experience, we can accept what he says because so many mystics have said the same thing.

As God penetrates me, I penetrate God in return....[91]
Where there is nothing but One, nothing but One is to be seen. [92]

In other words, Eckhart here refers to Nirvana. To borrow from a parable of Ramakrishna, the experience is like going into a factory filled with thousands of clay figures. "What a great variety you have here"—you say to the man in charge—"horses and dogs and men and children and birds." You take the multiplicity of the figures and the variety of their forms to be reality. But the manager responds, "They're all clay." *Clay* is the common reality—everything you see is one. "Where there is nothing but One, nothing but One is to be seen." This means we can perceive a world of apparent multiplicity but intuit behind it the radiating Light and omnipresent substance.

Unity of the Trinity Eckhart was a reverent monk, and he defended himself bravely against the charge of denying the truth of the Trinity, but to no avail. He didn't want to abandon the Church; he felt he could do more good by remaining a monk, not setting himself up as a rebel. He might have taken a different path and defied the Church, but it would have ended his effectiveness. For example, he might have been executed and then his books would not have been written, and his students would have lost their teacher. No doubt he was thinking more of them and of future generations than of himself. He had nothing to gain from the approval of the Church; he had already achieved his own spiritual enlightenment.

Eckhart never denied any of the traditional truths of the Church. He simply said that these were only the beginning:

> In this way the soul enters the unity of the Holy Trinity, but it may become even more blessed by going further, to the barren Godhead, of which the Trinity is a revelation.[93]

By "barren" he means *empty*—the Void, the Emptiness, the Nirvana we read of in Buddhism. Here in the waning years of the Middle Ages we have Eckhart's version of the Void: the barren Godhead; that is to say, the Godhead devoid of nonessentials, of all modifications. The light is untouched by the objects it shines upon, the air unsullied by the odors it may carry. Pure water is unaffected by the corruptions that intermingle with it—it remains the same throughout. If you take the corruptions away, the water is left intact. And so the Godhead is always the same—namely, barren. We do not like this word, although in this context it simply means essential, authentic, free from the nonessential. Although the Godhead always remains the same, our knowledge of It is not so. Hence when Eckhart writes of going further, to the Godhead, he alludes to our perception of It. It is always barren—that is, always pure—but our knowledge of It is colored by numerous other things, derived from our background, our personalities, our experiences.

> The difference between God and the Godhead is the difference between action and nonaction.[94]

Nonaction is superior to action; action is a phase of non-action, and *nonaction* is another word for the Absolute. The created world, the realm of becoming, of development in which we are involved, is the sphere of action and the domain of God, of creativity. To go beyond this to a timeless consciousness is to achieve a state of nonaction. This state does not imply dullness, nor rest in the sense of death. It is not the lethargy of tamas, but the tranquility of sattva. Nonaction signifies the peace that passes understanding.

16

 # The Sufis

Sufism, the mystical tradition of Islam, is one of the greatest and also one of the boldest. Even though Islam, like Judaism and Christianity, is not mystical in its received view, it has produced many genuine mystics.

One of its great spiritual teachers and visionaries, Muhammad Ibn al-Arabi, was born in 1165 in Moorish Spain. Let us examine a few of his teachings:

> It is necessary that you know Him ... not by learning nor by intellect.... By Himself He sees Himself.... There is no other, and there is no existence for any other than He.[95]

Ibn al-Arabi died in Damascus in A.D. 1240, so could not possibly have read Eckhart. Yet it seems as though he must have

All Are He

been influenced by Eckhart because of the parallel expression. Rather, it is the experience that brings the truth: "There is no other, and there is no existence for any other than He." This statement is characteristic of the Sufis, who reflect the truth of the Upanishads with a slightly different and somewhat bolder view than what we have heard from Western mystics: Not only is God the soul, but also the universe. Not only is God the Ruler, but He is humanity. Not only is God the Creator, but the created. Not only is God the Dramatist, but also the players.

> The existence of the beggar is His existence and the existence of the sick is His existence.... all of them are assuredly He.[96]

This echoes Christ's statement to his disciples: "Inasmuch as ye have done it unto one of the least of these my brethren, ye have done it unto me." (Matthew 25: 40) If you help a beggar in the proper spirit, not in the sense of superiority or indulgence but of humility, you are helping God in that person—perhaps God *is* that person. "The existence of the beggar is His existence." Again the idea that He is behind it all.

But isn't this *energy* he is talking about? Certainly it is. The

The Mystery Revealed

same energy is in the beggar and in the sun. It is the medium through which we function and that strengthens us, but there is something beyond.

> When the mystery ... is revealed to you.... Then you will see all your actions to be His actions ... though you do not thereby become He nor He you....[97]

The mystics tell us that when we merge into the Supreme Consciousness, we experience identity with the Divine. But when we emerge from that vision and return to our usual lives, we sense a distance between ourselves and God, even though we are now illumined.

> Just as he who dies the death of the body loses all his attributes.... He who knows himself sees his whole existence to be the Divine existence, but does not realize that any change has taken place in his own nature or qualities. For when you know yourself, "your I-ness" vanishes. [98]

For when the spiritual seeker comes into this illumined state it is himself—his true self that he embraces. In this state it is not a foreign country the seeker enters, rather, he discovers his own land the moment he arrives and "does not realize that any change has taken place in his own nature and qualities." It is like a dream, where the most fantastic things may happen to us and we take them for granted without surprise—a hint of what al-Arabi means. "For when you know yourself, 'your I-ness'"—your old individuality—"vanishes," and your other, truer individuality, and that of God, emerge as one.

> In the Beatific Vision God manifests himself to the elect in a general epiphany which, nevertheless, assumes various forms corresponding to the mental conceptions of God [we have cultivated].

If we have fashioned an image of the divine around Christ, for example, He can appear to us in that form, and the fullness of His being can be experienced through it. If this is what we want, we can have it. There is one Godhead, but many windows through which to view It. Continuing:

There is, then, one single epiphany which is multiple only by reason of the difference of forms by which it is received.... The Divine light pervades the beings of the elect and radiates from them, reflected as if by mirrors on everything around them.[99]

This light exists everywhere we turn. Wherever the enlightened person goes, he or she is like royalty. The light precedes such a person and illumines everything. He or she inherits the earth.

The famous Sufi poet Rumi believed that the forms of God are just as real as the Spirit, that the world of manifestation is just as sacred as the world of unmanifested Divinity. He speaks of deification:

When a fly is plunged in honey all the members of its body are reduced to the same condition.... Similarly one (who is absorbed in God) has no conscious existence or initiative or movement [apart from God].[100]

Some protest that it is the height of arrogance to say, "I am God." Rumi's defense is strong:

People imagine it is a presumptuous claim, whereas it is really a presumptuous claim to say "I am the slave of God." "I am God" is an expression of great humility. The man who says "I am the slave of God" affirms two existences, his own and God's, but he that says "I am God" has made himself nonexistent and has given himself up and says "I am God"—i.e., "I am naught, He is all: there is no being but God's." This is the extreme of humility and self-abasement.

This sheds further light on the meaning of Christ's "I am the Way, the Truth, and the Life."

In Rumi's "The Shepherd's Prayer" God reveals himself to Moses who has just criticized a shepherd for the way he worships:

"I have bestowed on every one a particular mode of worship. I have given everyone a peculiar form of expression." God doesn't want everyone to worship in the same way. Variety is integral to the design of the universe.

"Thou didst contrive this 'I' and 'we' in order to play the game of worship with Thyself." Again Rumi expands on the theme of the One and the Many, the same reality seen in two different modes in his poem "Love and Absence."

Rumi in his poem, "The Soul of Prayer," speaks of the immortality of the Soul: "The soul is unconditioned and infinite: it has neither beginning nor end." It was not created; anything that was created will have to have an end. Whatever began will have to conclude. Therefore if the soul is immortal it must always have existed and always will exist. If it was created it must necessarily be mortal and therefore have an end. You can't have it both ways.

We close on a universal note from Rumi's "The Shepherd's Prayer," which describes the Sufi ideal as well:

The religion of love is apart from all religions. The lovers of God have no religion but [Love] alone.

CONCLUSION

We have seen a great many testimonies to the universality of mysticism and to the idea of Oneness, of our unity with That, the Divine Reality or the Absolute, as described in Vedanta. Mystical experience is the direct personal experience of That. This Ultimate Reality is called by different names in different religious traditions: It is called Brahman by Hindus, Nirvana or the Void by Buddhists, Al Haqq (the Truth) by Sufis, and Union with God or the Beatific Vision by Christians.

Hopefully this introduction to fundamental Vedantic truths and confirmations from other sources will help to dispel the feeling that extreme statements by one mystic or another are explainable by personality differences or something of that kind. Perhaps we can strengthen our minds with the fortitude needed for spiritual life by realizing it's universality: all the great mystics seem to be speaking of the same thing. The Upanishads, the sayings of Christ, Buddha, Lao Tzu, Plotinus, Eckhart, and the Sufi masters living in different places and at different times have all discovered the same truths, providing us with an overwhelming presumption of certainty.

Let us imagine that they were writing for us, and that the Divine nature they experienced is likewise within us and realizable by us as well. Let us make their experience ours, and their transformed minds ours, so that our lives—to whatever degree we can attain—may be lived increasingly in the light of the illumination they knew.

NOTES AND REFERENCES

Part One - The Mysticism of India, An Overview

1. See more on Yoga in Chapter 4, p. 27.
2. *The Song of God: Bhagavad-Gita,* trans. with a commentary by Swami Prabhavananda and Christopher Isherwood. (Signet Classics, 2002), 36-38.
3. It has not been conclusively proven when Patanjali set down the Yoga Sutras, but yoga practice and philosophy predate this time by many centuries.

Part Two - The Upanishads: Thou Art That

4. *The Upanishads, Breath of the Eternal,* trans. Swami Prabhavananda and Frederick Manchester, (Hollywood: Vedanta Press, 1975), *Swetasvatara Upanishad, 187.*
5. Ibid., 187.
6. Ibid., 187-188.
7. Ibid., 188.
8. Ibid.
9. Ibid., 189.
10. Ibid., 195.
11. Ibid., 190.
12. Ibid., 75-76.
13. *The Upanishads,* trans. Juan Mascaro, (Great Britain: Penguin Books, 1965) 102.
14. *The Upanishads, Breath of the Eternal,* 76.
15. Ibid., 190.
16. Ibid.
17. Ibid.
18. Ibid., 191. See also the back cover for Eknath Easwaran's translation of this passage in *The Upanishads,* (Tomales, CA: Nilgiri Press, 1987), 8.

19. Ibid.
20. Ibid.
21. Ibid., 192.
22. Ibid., 193.
23. Ibid.
24. Ibid., 195.
25. Ibid.
26. *Holy Bible,* King James version, The First Epistle General of John, 4: 19.
27. *The Upanishads, Breath of the Eternal,* 195.
28. Ibid., 195-196.
29. Ibid., 196.
30. Ibid.
31. Ibid., 197.
32. Ibid., 198.
33. Ibid., 198-199.
34. Ibid., 201.
35. Ibid., 202.
36. Ibid.
37. Ibid., 202-203.
38. Ibid., 108.
39. Ibid., 109-110.
40. Ibid., 146.
41. Ibid., 142-143.
42. *Holy Bible*, John 7: 24.
43. *The Upanishads, Breath of the Eternal,* 144-145.
44. Ibid., 145-146.
45. Ibid., 23.
46. Ibid., 25.
47. Ibid., 25-26.
48. Ibid., 26.
49. Ibid., 26-27.
50. Ibid., 27.
51. Ibid.
52. Ibid., 27-28.
53. Ibid., 28.
54. Ibid.

55. Ibid., 28-29.
56. Ibid., 30-31.
57. Ibid., 31.
58. Ibid., 117.
59. Ibid., 31.
60. Ibid., 32.
61. Ibid., 33.
62. Ibid.
63. Ibid., 35.

Part Three - Brahman

64. Ibid., 38.
65. *The Complete Essays and Other Writings of Ralph Waldo Emerson*, ed. Brooks Atkinson (New York: Modern Library, 1950), 809.
66. *Holy Bible, Psalms* 139: 9-10

Part Four - Truth is One, Sages Call It by Many Names

67. See *Journey of the Upanishads to the West* by Swami Tathagatananda (New York: Vedanta Society of New York, 2002), Chapter 3, "Classical India and Classical Greece."
68. *Plotinus,* edited and translated by A. H. Armstrong. London: George Allen & Unwin, Ltd., 1953, 136-37; New York: The Macmillan Company, 1953, as cited in *The Teachings of the Mystics,* Walter T. Stace, (New York: Mentor/New American Library, 1960), 113.
69. The remaining quotations from Plotinus are from W. R. Inge's, *The Philosophy of Plotinus: The Gifford Lectures,* New York: Longmans, Green & Co., Inc., 3rd ed.,1929, Vol. II, 134-143, as cited in Stace's *The Teachings of the Mystics,* 114-121.
70. *The Teachings of the Mystics,* Walter T. Stace, (New York: Mentor/New American Library, 1960), 115.
71. Ibid.
72. Ibid., 115-116.
73. Ibid., 116.
74. Ibid.
75. Ibid., 117.
76. Ibid., 118.

77. Ibid., 119.
78. Ibid., 120.
79. Ibid.
80. Ibid., 121.
81. Ibid.
82. *The Way of Life,* Lao Tzu, R. B.Blakney trans., (New York: Signet Mentor, 1983), 101.
83. *Meister Eckhart, A Modern Translation,* Raymond B. Blakney, (San Francisco: Harper & Row, 1957), 214.
84. *Meister Eckhart,* Blakney, 206; Stace, 157.
85. Stace, 145.
86. *Meister Eckhart,* Blakney, 119; Stace, 147.
87. *Meister Eckhart,* Blakney, 120-121; Stace, 148.
88. *Walden,* Henry David Thoreau, Chaper 11, "Higher Laws"
89. *Meister Eckhart,* Blakney, 153; Stace, 153.
90. *Meister Eckhart,* Blakney, 181; Stace 153-154.
91. *Meister Eckhart,* Blakney, 193; Stace, 155.
92. *Meister Eckhart,* Blakney, 200; Stace, 155.
93. *Meister Eckhart,* Blakney, 200; Stace, 156.
94. *Meister Eckhart,* Blakney, 226.
95. Margaret Smith, *Readings from the Mystics of Islam,* New York: Pir Press, 1994, also cited in Stace, 211.
96. Stace, 211-212.
97. Ibid., 212.
98. Ibid.
99. Ibid., 212-213.
100. The remaining quotations are from *Rumi: Poet and Mystic* translated by R. A. Nicholson. London: George Allen & Unwin Ltd., 1950, as cited in Stace, 214 -219.

INDEX

A

advaita, 5, 71. *See also* impersonal approach to God
Arjuna, 21, 22–25
Atman, 4, 60, 100, 133, 135, 136, 147
  as identical with Brahman, 39
  defined, 18, 24–25, 100
Aurobindo, Sri, 6
avatar, 5, 6, 9, 71, 112

B

Bhagavad Gita, 3, 8, 9, 18, 36, 101
  described, 20–26
bhakti yoga, 21, 22
Blake, William, 73, 147, 157
bliss, 4, 40, 61, 86, 94
"Brahma", 127–129, 134–135, 139–140, 151, 158
Brahma, 130
Brahma Sutras, 3, 8
Brahman, 4, 22, 25, 45–46, 65, 68, 70–71, 74, 78, 85–86, 87, 88, 89, 98, 118, 123, 140, 143–144, 181. *See also* Self, the
  as personal and impersonal reality, 54–55, 71

  as tempter and deliverer, 130–135
  as ultimate reality, 39–40, 48–49
  defined, 19, 79, 127–129
  knowledge of, 87–88, 96, 98, 123
  OM as sound symbol of, 53
Brihadaranyaka Upanishad, 89–94, 132
Buddha, 5, 14, 26, 40, 47, 52, 62, 71, 99, 102, 103, 108, 112, 129, 141, 161, 170–171, 181
  experience of the absolute, 49, 60, 84, 133
  teachings of, 10, 51, 63, 77, 147
buddhi, 149
Buddhism, 5, 26, 76–77, 93, 143, 175

C

chakras, 97
Chandogya Upanishad, 87–88, 108–109, 161
Christ, Jesus, 10, 14, 26, 52, 62, 71, 99, 102, 103, 112, 115, 116, 117, 141, 147, 149, 179, 181

BIBLIOGRAPHY

Adiswarananda, Swami. *The Vedanta Way to Peace and Happiness.* Woodstock, VT: Skylight Paths Publishing, 2004.

Akhilananda, Swami. *Hindu Psychology, Its Meaning for the West.* London: Routledge & Kegan Paul Ltd., 1965.

The Bhagavad-Gita, Translated with Notes, Comments and Introduction by Swami Nikhilananda. New York: Ramakrishna-Vivekananda Center, 1952.

The Bhagavadgita, trans. by S. Radhakrishnan. London: George Allen & Unwin Ltd., 1970.

Eckhart, Meister. *Meister Eckhart, A Modern Translation,* Raymond B. Blakney. San Francisco: Harper & Row, 1957.

Emerson, Ralph Waldo. *The Complete Essays and Other Writings of Ralph Waldo Emerson,* ed. Brooks Atkinson (New York: Modern Library, 1950), 809.

How to Know God, The Yoga Aphorisms of Patanjali, trans. with a commentary by Swami Prabhavananda and Christopher Isherwood. Hollywood: Vedanta Press, 1996.

Lao Tzu, *The Way of Life,* trans. by R. B. Blakney. New York: Signet Mentor, 1983.

Nikhilananda, Swami. *The Gospel of Sri Ramakrishna.* New York: Ramakrishna-Vivekananda Center, 1942.

Reincarnation: An East-West Dialogue on Death and Rebirth, compiled and edited by Joseph Head and S. L. Cranston. New York: Julian Press, Crown Publishers, Inc., 1977.

Saradananda, Swami. *Sri Ramakrishna, The Great Master,* trans. by Swami Jagadananda. Mylapore: Sri Ramakrishna Math, 1952.

The Song of God: Bhagavad-Gita, trans. with a commentary by Swami Prabhavananda and Christopher Isherwood. New York: Signet Classics, 2002.

Stace, Walter T. *The Teachings of the Mystics.* New York: Mentor/New American Library, 1960.

Tathagatananda, Swami. *The Journey of the Upanishads to the West.* New York: The Vedanta Society of New York, 2002.

The Upanishads, Breath of the Eternal, trans. by Swami Prabhavananda and Frederick Manchester. Hollywood: Vedanta Press, 1987; New York: Mentor Books, 1975.

The Principle Upanishads, trans. by S. Radhakrishnan. London: George Allen & Unwin Ltd., 1968.

The Upanishads, A New Translation, by Swami Nikhilananda. New York: Harper & Brothers Publishers, 1956.

The Upanishads, Translated for the Modern Reader by Eknath Easwaran, Tomales, CA: Nilgiri Press, 1987, Reprinted 2003.

Vivekananda, Swami. *The Complete Works of Swami Vivekananda.* Calcutta: Advaita Ashrama, 1970.

Note: Because this listing was compiled and published after the author's passing, efforts have been made to ensure that the most vital texts used by the author and editor have been included.

ABOUT THE AUTHOR

PAUL HOURIHAN was born, raised, and educated in Boston where he earned an under-graduate degree from Harvard and a doctorate in American literature from Boston University. Over a period of 15 years he taught dozens of courses and gave many lectures in southern Ontario, Canada on the subjects of mysticism and great mystics such as Jesus Christ, Buddha and Ramakrishna.

For 45 years he was committed to the spiritual path and a serious student of the world's spiritual traditions, particularly India's Vedanta philosophy. His teacher, Swami Ritajananda, was a beloved and respected swami of the Ramakrishna Order of India.

In the last 20 years of his life, Dr. Hourihan wrote and prepared to publish his thought-provoking and compelling works that incorporate insights from his many years of meditative practice. This is the fifth of a dozen books on varying subjects, all with underlying spiritual themes.

He passed away peacefully in 2001 in Northern California where he lived with his wife, Anna, who continues to carry on his work.

AT VEDANTIC SHORES PRESS our goal is to help readers reach new shores of consciousness and Self-discovery by publishing the spiritual and thought-provoking works of Paul Hourihan.

Our creative biographies, novels and nonfiction books give a clear vision and practical understanding of spirituality and mysticism based on the teachings of the world's great mystical traditions, in particular Vedanta, the ancient system of thought of India.

We welcome our readers' views. If you'd like to comment on *Children of Immortal Bliss* or to learn more about the books and writings of Dr. Hourihan, visit our website at:

http://www.VedanticShoresPress.com

Or contact us:

Vedantic Shores Press
P.O. Box 493100, Redding, CA 96049
Tel: 530/549-4757   Fax: 530/549-5743
Toll-free: 866/549-4757 (U.S. only)
E-mail: info@vedanticshorespress.com

Also by Paul Hourihan and available from Vedantic Shores Press:

Mysticism in American Literature: Thoreau's Quest and Whitman's Self

Ramakrishna and Christ, The Supermystics: New Interpretations

Bill W., A Strange Salvation: A Biographical Novel Based on Key Moments in the Life of Bill Wilson, the Alcoholics Anonymous Founder, and a Probing of His Mysterious 11-Year Depression

Our publications may be ordered through your favorite bookseller or purchased directly from our website.